I0162008

Joshua, The Prince

A mystery unfolding in our generation

Rachelle C. Hood

Freedom LINE BOOKS

SEE YOU AT THE FREEDOM LINE.

Visit our website at www.freedomlinebooks.com.

Original and modified cover art by NaCDS and CoverDesignStudio.com

Acknowledgement—

Jeri, without your encouragement, this book would have never been written. Joshua would have remained a secret, confined to my private journals.

"And for the prince, because he is the prince, he may sit in it to eat bread before the Lord; he shall enter by way of the vestibule of the gateway, and go out the same way."
--- Ezekiel 44:3

"All the people of the land shall give this offering for the prince of Israel. Then it shall be the prince's part to give burnt offerings, grain offerings and drink offerings, and the drink offerings, at the feasts, the New Moons, the Sabbaths, and at all the appointed seasons of the house of Israel."
--- Ezekiel 44:16-17a

CONTENTS

Joshua, The Prince

Prologue

The purpose of this book is to introduce the reader to a little child named Joshua, who at this writing, is not yet born. As the Lord explained to me nearly 17 years ago, he is a promise, a deposit, a guarantee. He represents a promise of things to come in much the same way the Holy Spirit is a "deposit guaranteeing our inheritance" in Christ (Eph. 1:14, 2 Cor. 1:22, 2 Cor. 5:5).

Who am I? I am his mother. I am one of two women spoken of in Revelation 12:1-6—a multilayered Scripture passage with two fulfillments that occur more than 2,000 years apart. The child and I have remained a secret and a mystery until now. Our identities are being revealed to the "last generation"—the people who will experience the rapture and end of this present age.

Mary, the mother of our Lord and Savior, Christ Yeshua, fulfilled the first layer. She gave birth to the "male Child who will rule all nations with a rod of iron" (Rev. 12:5a). In the passage, she represents Israel more than 2,000 years ago. All other mentions of a male child in the text refer to the Lord's son, Joshua (Rev. 12:2, 4, 5b). I am the woman who will give birth to him during the time of the Antichrist. Symbolizing Israel at the close of the Church Age, I fulfill the second layer.

Lastly, there is a *third* layer. I am not the woman who flees into the wilderness and is preserved by God, away from the dragon—a 10-nation confederation ruled by the Antichrist (Rev. 12:6). Obviously, it is not Mary, because this event is during the Great Tribulation, more than 2,000 years after Mary's time. The "woman" is a remnant of Jews (and perhaps others of Hebrew descent), representing present-day Israel. The Lord will feed and nourish her—physically and spiritually—for 1,260 days or three and a half years in the wilderness.[1] After that period, she will weep tears of repentance. The Lord will hear her cries of remorse and regret. Messiah will forgive her transgressions and deliver her from every foe. Israel's cry from the wilderness will trigger Christ's Second Coming.

Two years before the Lord revealed to me that I was a symbol of Israel, He informed me that I was a "sign of the bride to come." By faith, I would "walk out" the preordained path of the Lord's mottled, tarnished spouse in my generation. His bride was spotted, wrinkled, and completely unaware—unmindful of her inglorious blemishes. She would have to be purified and refined as I was.

My life will also serve her in another way. At the very end of it, I will be a sign to her that she will be snatched up to heaven at a set and appointed time on God's calendar. Joshua and I will be caught up first as a pledge to her that she will soon follow. At that time, she will need this confirmation as never before. (My first book in the end-time trilogy, *The Spotted Bride*, discusses my life's call in great detail and its significance to the Lord's bride.)

Just as we believers have been given the gift of the Holy Spirit as a down payment—foretaste of a blessed life to come—the Lord placed a spiritual seed inside me as a foretaste of a gift to come. As believers, we know we have eternal life because of God's indwelling Spirit. His Spirit teaches, counsels, instructs, guides, admonishes, convicts, equips, enables, and comforts us. His work in, through, and for us serves as a wonderful witness to our

---

[1] Wilderness may be symbolic of an arduous, barren period or a literal desert.

souls that we have life everlasting. In this manner, the Holy Spirit is a foretaste of a future hope that we will spend eternity in God's glorious presence.

God placed a seed—the promise of Joshua—inside my womb. It is a foretaste, a hope of a promise to come. His presence within me works very much as a witness to me. It dispels all doubt, much like the Holy Spirit's presence does within me. I have discovered this seed is exactly the evidence I need to *know that I know that I know* what God has revealed to me about Joshua is as real as anything physical that I can see or touch.

Joshua is a child of tomorrow. He will be fully unveiled during Christ's millennial reign. We are given glimpses of him as a grown man in Ezekiel 44-46 and 48. There, he is referred to as the prince.

In this book, I will present the prince in the same way he was presented to me. God's revelations to me about him were progressive. That is, He did not disclose the child's identity and purpose to me all at once. It was done little by little, over a long period of time.

The Lord first introduced me to the idea of Joshua in a snippet of a dream. That dream was followed by a real-life, startling wonder meant to help me understand something related to a child would soon touch my life. A few days later, the Lord made His surprising request for a son. That request was followed by a divine visit from Him on October 31, 1997. That visit forever altered my life. As time passed, the Lord gave me and others, visions and dreams of this special child as He unfolded the Scriptures before us.

As discussed earlier, Mary's delivery of Christ, the Lion of Judah, fulfills the first layer of Revelation 12:1-6. In the Millennium, Christ will rule the world with an iron scepter (Rev. 12:5a). According to Scripture, after His death and resurrection, He ascended into heaven as the Perfect Man. As Man-God—100 percent Man and 100 percent God—He sits at the right hand of His Father. We, His Church, await His return. He is our Head (1 Cor. 11:3, Col. 1:18).

The birth of the second male child in the passage (Rev 12:2, 4 and 5b) serves as a symbol to the Body of Christ. The child is symbolic of how the Church will be delivered from the world. The Church will be caught up to heaven in the same manner Joshua will be caught up to God's throne (1 Thess. 4:15, 1 Cor. 15:51-52). In fact, the expression "caught up" that the Apostle Paul uses to describe the rapture of the Church in 1 Thessalonians 4:15-17 is the same one used in Revelation 12:5b to describe the snatching up of the male child.

In Greek, the term is "harpazo." It means "to seize upon with force," "to catch-up," "to snatch away." Latin translators used the verb "rapturo." This is where we get the English word "rapture." Joshua will be born approximately three and a half years before the Lord's Second Coming during the time of the Antichrist. Joshua is the son of the Son. The seven-head, ten-horn dragon, empowered by Satan, will attempt to destroy him (Rev. 12:4) and Christ's Body. Satan will not succeed in either case.

Many Bible commentaries identify Christ as the One who is caught up to God's throne in this passage. However, it is a clear teaching of Scripture that after His resurrection, Christ *ascended* into heaven in victory (Acts 1:9-11). He was not seized or snatched away from the devil's clutches as Joshua and the Church will be.

In natural childbirth, the delivery of the head precedes the delivery of the body. In like manner, Christ (our Head) born to Mary more than 2,000 years ago, precedes the delivery of His Body. Joshua's birth heralds the full and complete delivery of Christ's followers and the dawn of His millennial reign. Every person who composes this blessed assembly will be delivered at His Second Advent, but during a time of unprecedented upheaval. Scripture refers to it as the time of Jacob's trouble (Jer. 30:7). Prince Joshua's nativity will usher in an entirely new epoch in the Creator's dealing with mankind.

Chapter One
The Empty Baby Stroller

There was nothing in my life to indicate that I had been chosen by the Lord to bear a special child named Joshua until He made the request of me. In April 1997, He revealed to me that I was a "sign of the bride to come." It would take years for me to fully understand what that meant. Consequently, I was not expecting the divine visit that took place six months later.

Looking back, God gave me only one small indication that something unusual was in the offing. In a dream, I found myself on an auditorium stage. I was speaking and pushing an empty baby stroller. (I assume the stroller was empty because I never saw a baby.) I dreamt the detailed, three-scene dream on March 20, 1996. It still stands as the most terrifying nightmare of my life.

In the first scene, I exited the large stage, pushing the stroller. Behind stage, I was offered an obscene amount of money by an "admirer" dressed in a suit. He sat behind a big, ornate desk. I never saw his face. His identity was concealed. Repeatedly, I refused the check despite being told by the man's staff that the money was clean.

In the second scene, a caller came to visit. He appeared at my front door, ringing the doorbell, and knocking. He spoke sweetly in my husband Michael's voice, coaxing me to open the door.

"Come, let me in," he entreated.

I exited my bedroom in a long white nightgown. As I descended the staircase to check on the caller, I kept asking questions.

"Where is your key?"

"I forgot it," the voice said.

"How did you forget your key?" I asked stalling for time.

"I don't know. Just open the door."

I tried to pry open the blinds near the door to catch a glimpse of the caller. But it was as if the blinds had been glued together. Finally, they parted.

Standing at my front door was the most hideous beast I'd ever seen! Its long yellow fangs glistened in the dark as it turned to look at me peeping through the blinds. It was dressed in stylish jeans. The collar of the matching jean jacket was upturned, giving it a voguish look.

My mouth opened, but nothing came out. I screamed a silent scream. I was so petrified; I couldn't bring forth sound. I knew this brute had come to tear me apart.

Terrified out of my wits, I fled my home with my daughter Ryan and the empty baby stroller. We escaped out the back door. We jumped into a waiting car that had been sent by the Lord. We sped away. Later, God unmasked the fiend. It was a demonic spirit of covetousness and greed! At a future point, it would attempt to enter my life and assault it.

In the third scene, I found myself ascending a crystal spiral staircase—still pushing a baby stroller. As I rose, small-statured people with dark complexions and big almond-shape eyes surrounded me. A voice told me how much God loved me. For this reason, I thought they were angels. Three years would pass before God revealed they were Ethiopian Jews, and I was a descendant of these ancient people.

For days, I pondered the significance of the nightmare and the empty baby stroller. Despite repeated inquiries, the Lord would not reveal what either meant. He simply told me the dream was a forewarning of an evil to come. An attempt would be made by Satan to thwart my destiny with riches. The Lord would engineer my escape. He cautioned me not to succumb to the enemy's enticements.

Nine months after the dream I was offered a three-year, multimillion contract to join a U.S. company and dissolve my consulting firm, Inclusive Business Strategies, Inc. I declined. The Lord informed me the offer was just a foretaste of a larger temptation to come.

About the empty stroller, the Lord told me I would understand more with the passage of time. After several days of fruitless pondering, I pushed the dream out of my mind.

Chapter Two
An Invasion of Baby Strollers

Six months after the warning dream, I experienced an astonishing event. The event was a prelude to His visit that would occur 13 days later. Although this amazing incident boggled my mind for days and weeks to come, the Lord's visit still stands as the most remarkable wonder of my life.

At first, the Lord's feat—this disquieting experience occurring 13 days before His visit—was completely lost on me. I was too distraught to appreciate it. But in hindsight, the affair worked to strengthen and catapult my faith in Christ's ability to do *anything!*

In a confined space within a tightly condensed period, the Lord made my life intersect with countless strangers at very definitive seconds and moments in time to convey a divine message. The remarkable orchestration and precision required to accomplish the exploit still stuns me. Here's what happened.

On Saturday, October 18, 1997, I drove alone to the Haywood Mall in Greenville, South Carolina. I arrived around 11 o'clock in the morning. I wanted to pick up a few items and have lunch.

I pulled into a parking space near the mall entrance. As I exited my car, I noticed a woman removing a baby stroller from her car. She held the stroller in one arm and the baby in the other. I looked to my left. I spotted a different woman doing the same thing. I looked to my right. I saw another woman putting a stroller in her car. Nothing struck me as usual.

I walked inside the mall. I observed more mothers with strollers—right, left, up, down, here, there. I took the escalator up. I looked down. Everywhere I glanced, I saw women with strollers.

I was halfway through the mall, on the second floor, when it slowly dawned on me that something strange was happening, something impossible! In every direction I turned, the Lord made my eyes land on mothers pushing baby strollers!

Am I going crazy? Is this really happening? I tried my best to search out an elderly couple, a group of teenagers, a lone individual—ANYONE, ANYTHING—other than moms with baby strollers! I was confident the mall was filled with other people *without* strollers. But, where were they? I was not allowed to see them.

Completely discombobulated, I arrived at the food court on the other side of the mall. As I stood at the entrance of the food court and looked in, I saw a sea of mothers with baby strollers! I gasped. IS ANYONE ELSE SEEING THIS? Perhaps, if I had seen just one or two shoppers without a stroller, I could have collected myself. I didn't.

I spun around and turned my eyes downward. I began to push against the incoming patrons. I had to get out. I *ran* back the way I came. I purposefully kept my eyes on my feet. I bumped into people and things all along the way. I exited the mall and dashed to my car.

Outside the mall, I saw nothing but moms with baby strollers. Strollers, strollers, strollers everywhere. With my mind in a spin, I jumped in my car and sped home.

Now, I had two dots to connect—my pushing an empty baby stroller in a terrifying dream and an "invasion" of moms pushing their babies in strollers at a mall.

"Lord, what's going on? What's happening here?" The Lord would not reveal more. Even though I entreated and prodded Him, He remained completely silent on the matter.

Chapter Three
A Wild Request

On the morning of October 26, 1997, during my time alone with the Lord, He suddenly interrupted our conversation with a pronouncement. It took me completely by surprise. I stopped midsentence. *Surely, I did not hear Him correctly.*

"What did you just say?" I asked.

"I want a son." I *had* heard correctly! Still, I doubted because the declaration was so unexpected and extraordinary.

At first, I was quiet. My mind sputtered. I was not exactly sure what I had to do with His desire for a son. Was He just sharing a hidden, secret longing with an intimate friend? Finally, I realized it was a request!

Not fully understanding it all, I told Him my life was not my own. He had redeemed me. I belonged to Him. In that setting, He said nothing more and I certainly did not push for details. At that moment, I made no connection with the alarming baby-stroller dream or my bizarre mall excursion.

I rose from bed to prepare for church. That day, I distinctly remember wearing a red business suit. Initially, wearing that suit symbolized nothing to me. Hours later, I understood the significance of the color.

That Sunday morning, Pastor Nelson of the First Baptist Church of Greer, took his sermon text from the second chapter of Philippians:

> *Let this mind be in you which was also in Christ Jesus, who being in the form of God, did not consider it robbery to be equal with God, but made Himself of no reputation, taking the form of a bondservant, and coming in the likeness of men. And being found in appearance as a man, He humbled Himself and became obedient to the point of death, even the death of the cross (Phil. 2:5-9).*

After Pastor Nelson's moving message, I quietly rose from my pew and walked to front of the church. I was the only one who came forward. Alone, I knelt before the altar and wept. The entire congregation was quiet. I heard not a whisper, cough, or sneeze. Weeping there, I told the Lord: "If I understood You correctly this morning, my answer to You is 'Yes.'" That momentous morning is described in the journal excerpt below.

October 26, 1997

The Mind (Attitude) of Christ

I should record this while it is still fresh in my mind. It may prove significant later. This morning I had a very odd conversation with the Lord. I do not know that I understood Him correctly. He let His desires be known to me. He asked me for the most incredible thing—a son!

I answered that my life was not my own. It was His. I had been bought with a price. Not my will, but His will be done. Then, I ate breakfast, dressed, and headed to church in the pouring rain.

During the worship service, the Spirit's presence was especially strong. I could not stop crying. Pastor Nelson, full of the Spirit, gave a powerful sermon on the mind of Christ. He spoke from Philippians 2:5-9, a passage that has significant meaning to me. He supposed we all required an attitude adjustment. We all needed to have the attitude of Christ. He gave it all.

He, who was equal with God and who was God, humbled Himself. He left all His majesty and splendor in heaven to become a Man-Servant. He emptied Himself—became nothing so that we may have life abundantly and eternally. Totally obedient to the Father, Jesus became sin for us.

I tried to imagine what it was like for the Lord when He became sin for us. At that moment, for the first time in all eternity, He was separated from His Father. That had to be the most dreadful, agonizing part of the crucifixion, worse than being beaten until He was unrecognizable.

"What shall I ever withhold from Him?" I asked myself. "Is there anything too great that He could ask of me?" I concluded if something was within my power to give Him, I would give it. I would not withhold anything from the One who gave me everything.

That day, I agreed to make a sacrifice of a different kind. Dressed in my red suit—the color of love and passion—I offered my body to the Lord for Him to use as He saw fit. I fully belonged to Him. Despite being completely open to the Lord's will, I was not the least bit prepared for His next move.

Chapter Four
The Visit

On October 31, 1997, at exactly 4 a.m., I received a visit from the Lord. We were in the middle of what I thought was a lively conversation when He said, "I want to come to you."

"Then come, Lord, come," I said without hesitation.

I fully expected Him to come to me in a spate of spine-tingling shivers as He had done so many times before. Sometimes the chills traveled up and down my frame. Other times, they engulfed my whole body at once. During the latter encounters, my entire body would just vibrate. Never would I ever imagine He would appear in my bedroom!

The room was dark. I laid in the bed with my eyes closed, waiting for the shivers. But instead, I heard a soft thump near the foot of my bed. It sounded as if a throw pillow had fallen to the floor. But how could that be? I hadn't move.

I waited quietly, not confident anything was amidst until I heard another, louder sound—MOVEMENT! He was moving toward where I lay. My eyes popped open in the unlit room. My mind screamed, *He's here! He's in the room!*

Mere seconds later, the entire room was engulfed in brilliant light. I closed my eyes. Suddenly, I began to experience an electrical pulsating sensation that engulfed my whole body.

There was no pain, just a continuous pulsating electric feeling that encased my whole being. Facing my bedroom window, I dared not try to turn around, open my eyes, or lift my head from the pillow.

Inexplicably, though my eyes were closed, I could see everything that was happening. During the pulsating phenomenon, I saw a laser of bright light travel through the center of my being. It started at the top of my head and exited between my legs. Not knowing what else to do, I prayed as it was happening.

Afterward, two massive hands enveloped mine and began to pull me up from the bed. I *felt* His hands! At this point, I began to shout in my spirit, *I don't want to see Your face! I don't want to see Your face!* I was confident if I saw His face, I would die. I knew from Scripture that no earthly being had ever seen God's face and lived. I have since learned this may not be true (See Exodus 24:9-11).

At the very end of the event—with my eyes still sealed—I saw a mammoth Figure of bright light hovering just above the head of my bed. I knew the Figure was God, the Father. I saw only His head and torso. I saw and felt when He gently kiss the crown of my head. Then, He disappeared. The brilliant light went with Him.

When my eyes sprang open, my room was dark as it had been before. I noted the time. It was 4:49 a.m. I fell back to sleep. When I rose in the morning, I had completely forgotten the encounter. I didn't remember it until our evening walk. The Lord confirmed that He had come. His visit would forever change my life.

Four months later, stepping out of the shower, I caught a glimpse of my complete figure in my bathroom's full-length mirror. My mouth dropped. I saw a circular, protruding mound in the middle of my stomach!

I had not used my master bathroom to take a shower since my parents came for an extended visit to escape the brutal Michigan winter. I had given them my master suite. During their four-month stay I slept on an air mattress in my home office. Michael also had a master suite, although it wasn't as large as mine. (His epic snoring precipitated these sleeping arrangements.) I used his bathroom during those four months. As the Lord would have it, I could only see the area above my chest—my shoulders and head—in Michael's bathroom mirror.

I knew the mound was connected to the Lord's visit four months earlier. I just stood there rubbing my stomach and saying over and over: "*This* is a BIG IDEA! *This* is a BIG IDEA!" I felt the expression was not my own, but a phrase the Holy Spirit had me speak.

Clearly, I had become engaged in something way beyond my human comprehension, something that would have enormous implications for my life and the Body of Christ. God was saying to me: "Don't try to understand what is happening at this point. You can't. The idea is too big. Just believe."

Over the course of time, I came to embrace the idea of a little, yet-to-be-born child named Joshua deposited inside my womb. But so many questions went unanswered those first few weeks and months. Some questions were not answered for years. Among those was God's timing.

Why had He picked October 31 to plant Joshua inside my womb? "Could You have picked a worse date?" I complained time and again to the Author and Orchestrator of All Space and Time. "How could You associate something so special and sacred with Halloween?" Three years later, I learned about All Saints' Eve—the predecessor of Halloween.

July 19, 2000

All Saints' Eve

While doing some research for Jeri, I came across an intriguing bit of information. It answered a basic question I've had for nearly three years. Why did the Lord choose October 31 to place Joshua inside my womb?

If I had to pick my least favorite day of the year, it would be October 31, because of what the day symbolizes in Western culture. It is a secular holiday set aside to commemorate death, darkness, and the underworld. In 1984, the year I invited Christ into my life, I stopped celebrating Halloween.

According to a book on cults and religions, authored by Josh McDowell and Don Stewart, Halloween traces to a very sacred church tradition:

> *Before the introduction of Christianity to these lands, the celebration of death was not called Halloween. Halloween is a form of the designation "All Hallows Eve," a holy evening instituted by the church to honor all the saints of church history. While All Hallows Eve began as a strictly Christian holiday, the pagan influences from earlier traditions gradually crept in while the church's influence waned.[2]*

The Old English Century Dictionary further corroborates McDowell and Stewart's explanation: Halloween—All hallow eve; hallow; halga, definitive form of halig (see Holy) in sense a "holy person,

---

[2]Josh McDowell and Don Stewart, *Understanding the Cults: Handbook to Today's Religions.* Thomas Nelson Publishers, 1996, p. 261.

hence saint." [Halloween is] the evening of October 31, which is followed by All Saints' Day, or All hallows; Halloween is now generally celebrated with fun-making and masquerading.[3]

At last, I understood why God chose October 31 to bestow Joshua. Originally, Halloween was a sacred day in Christendom—a day to honor all the saints of church history for their faith in Christ. All Saints' Eve is the holy evening (or eve) before All Saints Day, November 1. Satan, as he does with all things, perverted the day's meaning. Among many believers of our generation, Halloween is viewed as wicked and pagan. However, in heavenly realms the day is still hallowed for its original meaning.

Further, aside from the interesting play on words that the Lord revealed to me shortly after the All Saints' Eve discovery[4], I uncovered yet another reason for the October date. It is connected to the Jewish calendar. This will be discussed in Chapter 13.

---

[3]William Dwight Whitney, *The Century Dictionary: An Encyclopedic Lexicon of the English Language, Volume 12,* The Century Company, 1989, pp. 275-276.
[4]*I am an Eve to the Second (or Last) Adam. Scripture refers to Christians, followers of Jesus Christ, as saints. Thus, I am a type of All Saints' Eve.*

Chapter Five
Sharing My Report

For days, I laid awake in bed trying to sort out the practical implications of what was happening to me and what my next move should be. Of course, the Lord was not a participant in these marathon hand-wringing sessions. He wanted me to rest in His care and Providence. At this stage of my walk with Him, I did not know how to rest amid what I saw as pending calamity. I wanted answers and I wanted them fast. *Where is this train headed? When will it crash? Who can I tell? Who will believe me? What will people think? Will I have to quit my job? How will I explain this to Michael—a nonbeliever!* On and on I went, night after night.

My first step was to have an ultrasound to confirm the pregnancy. That occurred two weeks after discovering the bump. I told Michael I was going in for the test—nothing more. He quietly awaited the results, knowing he had a vasectomy 16 years earlier.

The test came back negative—no evidence of anything *physical* inside my womb. However, the doctor acknowledged I looked four months pregnant as he poked and kneaded my stomach. Michael joked that I had "dodged a bullet." I never again broached the subject with him. I did not have to. Four weeks later, God separated us. Neither of us saw the separation coming. Five years later, we divorced.

Jeri Dotson was the first person I chose to tell. She was my best friend. By that time, we had known each other for 12 years. We were like sisters. Even still, I shared my story with her hesitantly and haltingly. She believed my report without question or reservation.

Emboldened by Jeri's response, I told Suzanne Eustache next. She was my live-in housekeeper as well as a close friend. She helped me raise my daughter Ryan, from age two. She had known me for 14 years. Like Jeri, she knew that my walk with the Lord was close and intimate.

The first thing she asked was to see me unclothed. She carefully examined my stomach. With her finger, she gently traced the dark vertical line running from my navel to my pubis. Having seen me unclothed before, she knew the line had not been there previously. She quietly nodded her head in belief.

Ryan was next to learn of the wonder. At the time, she was only 16 years old. Sometimes she believed wholeheartedly. At other times, she doubted. By the time she was 18 years old, however, the Lord had given her enough dreams about Joshua to fuel a steadfast belief in him.

In her very first dream of him, the Lord presented Joshua as a precocious baby orator. As she tickled his tummy and conversed with him, he repeated back to her—in baby gurgles—every word and phrase she spoke. In another dream, he was a dancing toddler. He danced with His Father. Both wore jeans and matching plaid, lumberjack shirts. The Lord created the scene in such a way that she could see them only from the neck down. Neither of them danced very well. In still another dream, Ryan helped Joshua get ready for a formal event. He was about five years old. They were running late because she kept him out too long. She quickly dressed him in a yellow suit with short pants and a little black bow tie.

In her most intriguing dream of all, I was present. In that dream, Joshua was dressed like an Egyptian. Sitting in a highchair, he wore a gold-encrusted Egyptian headdress and a gold collar around his neck. He also wore little gold harem pants. His chubby feet were bare, and his round belly exposed. Dark eyeliner encircled his eyes.

I was also dressed like an Egyptian. I stood next to his highchair, attired in a similar Egyptian headdress. I also wore a gold collar around my neck. Every time I opened my mouth in a silent scream, he opened his. We both screamed silently and in sync as if in labor.

At the time of this dream, Ryan and I lived in Memphis, Tennessee—a city patterned after the ancient city of Memphis, Egypt. In the Old Testament, Egypt is a place of bondage and Canaan is the Promised Land. Under the New Covenant of Jesus Christ, the world is symbolic of Egypt, a place of oppression and captivity. Heaven represents the Promised Land.

The Lord explained our Egyptian attire pointed to Him, one day, calling Joshua out of Egypt—out of the world to heaven—just as He called out Moses and the children of Israel from Egyptian bondage to the Promised Land (Ex. 4:22-23, Hos. 11:1). Likewise, according to Matthew 2:15, the Lord was called out of Egypt as a boy to return to Israel after the death of King Herod. (The spiritual significance of Memphis, Tennessee and how God used the city symbolically in our lives is discussed in greater detail in Book One, *The Spotted Bride*.)

The Lord used this dream and many others to convince Ryan that one day she would have a little brother. In time, she welcomed and embraced the idea with her whole heart. She looked forward to it.

A few weeks after the baby bump discovery, I was moved to share my mindboggling story with two trusted colleagues—April Kelly and Dora Canals. Both women are followers of Christ. April fully accepted my report. Dora eventually rejected it, though the Lord gave her mother a dream about Joshua that she relayed to me. To this day, I have never met Dora's mother. I only know her name is Sarah.

March 3, 1999

Sarah's Dream: A Special Baby

After I relayed Suzanne's dream about Joshua to April and Dora, Dora told me a peculiar dream her mother Sarah had about a baby. "I don't know why it didn't occur to me to tell you about this dream until now," she said.

According to Dora, the dream excited her mother because it seemed so real. Early the next morning, Sarah called Dora from Miami, Florida. She tracked her down at work in Spartanburg, South Carolina to tell her the dream.

In Sarah's dream, Dora was holding a shining, glowing baby boy. Clearly, he was no ordinary child. According to Sarah, the glowing infant had shocking white hair and blue eyes. I was certain, as was Dora at the time, that she was holding Joshua.

Interestingly, another friend of mine dreamt I delivered a baby who looked quite like the one in Sarah's dream. Their descriptions of Joshua perplex me—not his glowing complexion. That is symbolic of him being the Lord's child. But his white hair and blue eyes puzzled me. I am Black. My eyes and hair are dark brown. How could this be? I wondered.

Previously, I concluded Joshua being described as having white hair and blue eyes in my other friend's dream is because she has three blonde, blue-eyed sons. Her entire family is blonde. I assumed this fact colored her dreams.

But Sarah is Cuban-American. If race colored dreams, why didn't this Latino woman dream about a baby with darker features? How could they both have dreamt with such peculiar specificity? Neither woman has ever met the other.

The Lord has assured me Joshua will look very much like the two of us. Maybe, in these dreams his odd and striking features symbolize how rare or different he'll be.

I have turned everything over and over in my mind. It's all too much for me to understand, to grasp. I must wait on the Lord. In time, He will reveal more.

A few weeks after the ultrasound, all hell broke loose in my life. I was suddenly thrust into a level of spiritual warfare I had never experienced before. Trouble and distress, all at once, overwhelmed my life. Both my work life and home life flipped upside-down.

In an unprecedented, unexpected move of the Lord, Ryan and I had to flee our South Carolina home. I had an inkling something big and foreboding was on the horizon, but I just didn't know what it was. The Lord had warned me: "I did not come to bring peace! I came to divide." And divided us, He did.

Ryan and I relocated to Detroit, Michigan to live with my parents. Michael moved to Chicago, Illinois, where he worked in movie and television production. Suzanne moved to Wichita, Kansas to care for her ailing sister-in-law, who later died of cancer.

It all happened within the span of just seven days! One week we were all living together under one roof with no thought of separation. The next week, God split us. During a 30-minute telephone conversation, He sold our home! Our family life, as we knew it, was over. (The reason for the split is discussed at length in Book One, *The Spotted Bride*.)

As a consequence of moving in with my parents, they were the next ones in line to learn of the mystery. My concern was they would see my stomach grow and, in time, ask for an explanation. At that juncture, I did not know the size of the baby bump would remain the same for the next 17 years! I decided, after much prayer, to tell them the whole truth before being asked. My report sounded so unbelievable; I was convinced they would think I had lost my mind. My stomach was in knots on the day I decided to tell them. I remember the event as if it were yesterday.

One evening I waited until just the three of us were alone in the house. I invited them to join me in the living room. I sat in the middle of the sofa. My mother sat in an oversized cushioned chair to my right, near the big picture window. My father sat to the left of me on the sofa. I didn't know how to start. They waited. Finally, I stammered, stuttered, and stumbled through my story. I wept throughout the entire confession.

My father looked at my mother without a hint of condemnation on his face. I will always be grateful for my mother's measured response, following a long silence that seemed to fill every crevice of the room: "Nothing is impossible with God." That was it. The matter was settled. We all rose and resumed what we were doing before our talk.

From that day forward, neither of them ever raised the subject again, not even on their deathbeds. I can say without hesitation that their treatment of me remained unchanged. They were kind and loving before the report and after it.

Chapter Six
The Mystery of Revelation 12:1-6

1 A woman clothed with the sun, with the moon under her feet, and on her head a garland of 12 stars. 2 Then being with child, she cried out in labor and in pain to give birth. 3 And another sign appeared in heaven: behold, a great, fiery red dragon having seven heads and 10 horns, and seven diadems on his heads. 4 His tail drew a third of the stars of heaven and threw them to the earth. And the dragon stood before the woman who was ready to give birth, to devour her child as soon as it was born. 5 She bore a male Child who was to rule all nations with a rod of iron. And her child was caught up to God and His throne. 6 Then the woman fled into the wilderness, where she has a place prepared by God, that they should feed her there one thousand two hundred and sixty days (Rev. 12:1-6).

In the spring of 1998, the Lord began to unfold Scripture to me about Joshua. He began with Revelation 12:1-6. More than a year would pass before I realized the passage was layered. It pointed to more than one fulfillment. The passage involves *two* women in labor, giving birth to *two* male children more than 2,000 years apart. Both women represent Israel at *two* different points in history.

July 22, 1999

Who is the Woman in Revelation 12?

Many Biblicists believe the woman described in Revelation 12:1-6 is a symbol of Israel. She is "clothed with the sun, with the moon under her feet." On her head is a garland of 12 stars. The garland of 12 stars represents Israel's 12 tribes.

However, the description also indicates the woman is a believer in Jesus Christ. She is "clothed with the sun." This signifies she is covered in His righteousness. All believers are clothed in His righteousness. Malachi 4:2 refers to Christ—the Light of the World— as the Sun of Righteousness: "But to you who fear My name the Sun of Righteousness shall arise with healing in His wings; and you shall go out and grow fat like stall-fed calves."

The expression "under her feet" connotes "controlled by" or "subject to." Since the Hebrews used the moon to establish their times and seasons, the phrase "moon under her feet" suggests the Lord has fixed or established the times and seasons of the last days, including the Church Age's end, around the woman and the birth of her child.

What most people do not realize is that the passage refers to two separate women, symbolic of Israel, more than 2,000 years apart. One is Mary, the mother of Jesus. The other is a woman, symbolic of Israel at the end of the Church Age.

The woman, symbolic of Israel at the end of the age, will be caught up to heaven along with the child. The "woman" who flees into the desert to a place prepared for her by God, where she will be taken care of for 1,260 days or 3½ years, is a surviving remnant of Jews (and conceivably others of Hebrew descent) during the Great Tribulation. She also symbolizes Israel.

Just as there are two women in Revelation 12:1-6, there are two male children. There are four mentions of a male child within the passage: verses 2, 4, 5a and 5b. Only Revelation 5a refers to Jesus Christ. The other three verses refer to *another* child, a son born to the second woman during the time of the Antichrist.

The child in verse 2, "Then being with child, she cried out in labor" refers to an ordinary child ("teknon"). The child in verse 4, "And the dragon stood before the woman who was ready to give birth, to devour her child as soon as it was born" also refers to an ordinary child ("teknon"). The child described in verse 5a, "She bore a male child who was to rule all nations with a rod of iron" refers to the divine Son ("huios"), whom we know to be Jesus Christ (Ps. 2:9, Rev. 2:27, 19:15). The last mention of a male child in verse 5b, "And her child was caught up to heaven" refers to a regular baby ("teknon"), not the divine Baby of 5a ("huios").

Even without the different Greek renderings, one can see the passage cannot refer solely to Yeshua, because He ascended into heaven as a fully-grown adult—the Perfect Man-God. Yeshua was not snatched up to God's throne as a baby!

We see the suggestion of a second woman even more clearly in Micah 5:3. The verse speaks of Messiah uniting the house of Judah and the house of Israel/Ephraim at the end of the age "when she who is in labor has given birth." This cannot be Mary. It is more than 2,000 years *after* her time:

Therefore He shall give them up, until the time that she who is in labor has given birth; then the remnant of His brethren shall return to the children of Israel. And He [Christ] shall stand and feed his flock in the strength of the Lord, in the majesty of the name of the Lord His God; and they shall abide, for now He shall be great to the ends of the earth; and this One shall be peace (Mi. 5:3-5, Amplified Bible).

In John MacArthur's commentary about this puzzling passage, he says:

Regathering of the "remnant of His brethren" did not occur at the First Advent but is slated for the Second Advent (cf. Is. 10:20-22; 11:11-16). Nor can "return" speak of Gentiles, since it cannot be said that they "returned" to the Lord. Rather, the context of 5:3-4 is millennial and cannot be made to fit the First Advent.[5]

MacArthur deduces "she who is in labor" must be the nation of Israel. He is partially correct. "She who is in labor" is a literal woman at the end of the age, who symbolizes Israel. She will give birth to a second male child, Joshua, the Son's son—named *by* His Father *for* His Father. (The name Yeshua contracts to Joshua in Greek and English.)

Joshua's birth, like his Father's, will usher in a new epoch in God's dealing with mankind. His birth and snatching up will signal the beginning of the Great Tribulation, the last three and a half years of the present age. Joshua's birth also heralds the 1,000-year reign of Christ when the whole house of Israel and the Church will be united under Yeshua Ha-Mashiach!

The first woman in Revelation 12, Mary, who gave birth to Jesus Christ, gave birth to the Head of the Church. That delivery marked Christ's First Advent as the Suffering-Servant Savior. After His crucifixion, burial, and resurrection, Yeshua ascended into heaven. He is presently seated at the right hand of God (Romans 8:34, Acts 7:55-56). The Church awaits His Second Advent. At the end of the Church Age, after more than 2,000 years of building His Church (or Body), Christ will have a son of His own (vv. 2, 4 and 5b). The *second* woman in Revelation 12 will give birth to him.

According to Scripture, a seven-head, 10-horn dragon will try to devour Joshua (Rev 12:4). But the child will be caught up to God's throne in the same manner the Church (Christ's Body) will be caught up to heaven (1 Thess. 4:15, 1 Cor. 15:51-52). In a

---

[5]*John MacArthur, The MacArthur Study Bible (NKJ), Word Publishing, 1997, p. 1,304.*

manner of speaking, Joshua's birth and catching up embodies the full and complete deliverance of Christ's Church (Body).

Satan is the power behind the metaphorical seven-head, 10-horn dragon. The frightful figure symbolizes the dominion of six past worldly kingdoms that dominated Israel (i.e., Egypt, Assyria, Babylon, Medo-Persia, Greece, and Rome) as well as the Revived Roman Empire (i.e., the seventh head)[6], which will do the same under Satan's sway. The 10 horns on the beast represent a 10-nation confederacy (i.e., the eighth and final earthly kingdom), under the Antichrist's dictatorship during the last three and a half years of the age.

Joshua represents a child of tomorrow, a hope of the future. He will be raised during Christ's millennial reign. Hence, his birth signals the death, the complete destruction of Satan's millennia-long rule over the Gentile empires of the world. No wonder the Satan-inspired dragon will seek to destroy him.

Israel's Generations Laboring to Give Birth

The key to understanding Revelation 12:1-6 is to view the passage as the dramatic culmination of Israel, at last, finalizing what God always intended her to complete—an important birth or "delivery" in the earth. God always intended Israel—Judah and Ephraim—to be a light to the Gentiles. Israel was meant to be a testimony of God's greatness and goodness. She was to show the nations of the world that her God is earth's only Savior, the Messiah. The Bible, metaphorically, employs the idea of Israel "giving birth" to encapsulate this important responsibility.

---

[6] *It is this author's opinion that we are witnessing the "Revived Roman Empire" in its embryonic state within the United Nations, headed by the United States of America and other western nations.*

At the end of the Church Age, a woman representing Israel *will* give birth to a literal male child, as prophesied in Micah 5:3-5 and depicted in Revelation 12:1-2. But just as important, both Ephraim and Judah (Jews) will accomplish important deliveries in the earth as well. Afterward, the two houses will join as a united Israel under Messiah.

Ephraim: As it turns out, more than 2,000 years after Christ's resurrection and ascension, many of Ephraim's descendants are hidden in the mostly-Gentile Church throughout the world. They know nothing of their Hebrew heritage.

While many of Ephraim's descendants are completely unaware of their Hebrew roots, God isn't. Presently, they are a hidden treasure within Christ's body. Near the very end of the age, He will call them out of the graveyard of the nations, breathe life into them, and raise them up as a mighty army for His glory. As God's firstborn, they will lead the Church in taking the Gospel of Christ Yeshua to the ends of the earth.

Judah: During her three and a half years in the wilderness, a remnant of Jews (and likely others of Hebrew descent), whom the Lord will preserve for Himself, will come to realize that Yeshua is, indeed, Messiah. In repentance, they will cry out to Him to be saved. At that moment, they will be united with Ephraim, their Christian brethren, in the belief that Christ is the world's One and Only Redeemer. They will summon Yeshua Ha-Mashiach to a near-desolate planet, to deliver them. He will answer their cry.

Until that point, Jews as a people, will have had a long history of disobeying God and rejecting His commands. For more than 2,000 years, they have refused to accept Christ Yeshua as

Messiah. There is a reason for this. They were blinded until the "fullness of the Gentiles has come in" (Romans 11:25-26). At the end of the Great Tribulation, like Ephraim, Jews will see and receive Christ as their Sin Bearer.

The Prophet Isaiah compared the nation's stubborn refusal to be a light to Gentile nations to a woman unable to give birth:

> *As a woman with child is in pain and cries out in her pangs, when she draws near the time of her delivery, so have we been in Your sight, O Lord. We have been with child, we have been in pain; we have, as it were, brought forth wind; we have not accomplished any deliverance in the earth, nor have the inhabitants of the world fallen" (Is. 26:17-18).*

However, the world will be pushed closer to that long-awaited, monumental delivery during the reign of the cruel and merciless Antichrist. It will be a time of unprecedented horror for Israel (and the world). Scripture calls it the time of Jacob's trouble:

> *Ask now, and see, whether a man is ever in labor with child? So why do I see every man with his hands on his loins like a woman in labor, and all faces turned pale? Alas! For that day is great, so that none is like it; and it is the time of Jacob's trouble …. (Jer. 30:6-7).*

At one point in history, Ephraim was as obstinate as Judah in refusing to obey God's instructions and commands. Employing the woman-in-labor metaphor, the Prophet Hosea writes: *"The iniquity of Ephraim is bound up; his sin is stored up. The sorrows of a woman in childbirth shall come upon him. He is an unwise son, for he should not stay long where children are born"* (Hos. 13:12-13).

Where children are born refers to the birth canal. Stubborn Ephraim, at this point in history, was unwise in its unwillingness to obey God and move through to birth—to become a witness nation for Him in the earth. Bible commentator, John MacArthur, writes: *"By long deferring a 'new birth' with repentance, the nation was like a child remaining in the canal dangerously long and risking death."*[7]

God's plan for purging the rebels from among Ephraim was to send His people back to Egypt in slave ships. This happened during the Transatlantic Slave Trade that lasted more than four centuries. (For a detailed discussion of this misadventure, we refer the reader to Book Two, *Two Hidden Treasures*, in the Spotted Bride Series.) In captivity, many of Ephraim's descendants finally found their way back to God through Christ. Just before Christ's Second Advent, this Hebrew progeny, in exile for hundreds of years, will be raised up as a mighty multitude of witnesses for Him.

Speaking of Judah's Babylonian exile that foreshadowed the exile of Israel's descendants in a latter-day Babylon known as "Babylon the Great" (i.e., United States), Micah prophesied:

> ... For the pangs have seized you like a woman in labor. Be in pain and labor to bring forth, O daughter of Zion, like a woman in birth pangs. For now you shall go forth from the city, you shall dwell in the field, and to Babylon you shall go. There you shall be delivered .... (Mi. 4:9b-10a).

Israel's Special Deliverance for the World

During the time of Jacob's trouble, two-thirds of the nation of Israel will be destroyed by the Antichrist (Zech. 13:8-9). However, God will preserve a faction of Jews for Himself (Rev. 12:6, 14). He will feed and nurture this holy remnant, identified

---

[7] *John MacArthur, The MacArthur Study Bible (NKJ), Word Publishing, 1997, p. 1,265.*

previously as the *third* "woman" in Revelation 12:1-6 (see Prologue). The Lord will supply her physical needs. But more importantly, He will nourish her spiritually with His truth during her 1,260 days in the wilderness (Rev. 12:6, 14).

Finally, she will cry out to Christ in repentance. Rest assured that her call will summon Messiah to a nearly destroyed world. He will end the mayhem for God has promised to all who love Jerusalem and mourn for Israel's deliverance: *"Shall I bring to the time of birth, and not cause a delivery?" says the Lord. Shall I who cause delivery shut up the womb?" says your God (Is. 66:9).*

When Christ returns to answer Israel's cry for deliverance in the wilderness, He will bring a complete and utter end to all her foes:

> *"For it shall come to pass in the day," says the Lord of hosts, "that I will break his yoke from your neck, and will burst your bonds; foreigners will no more enslave them" (Jer. 30:8).*

> *Now also many nations have gathered against you, who say, "Let her be defiled, and let our eye look upon Zion." But they do not know the thoughts of the Lord, nor do they understand His counsel; for He will gather them like sheaves to the threshing floor (Mi. 4:11-12).*

> *"... Jacob shall return, have rest and be quiet, and no one shall make him afraid. For I am with you," says the Lord, "to save you; though I make a full end of all nations where I have scattered you, yet I will not make a complete end of you" (Jer. 10b-11a).*

Israel—Part of Christ's Body

Despite what the Church teaches, anyone suffering or martyred for the cause of Christ Yeshua—Gentile or Jew—during the Great Tribulation are an integral part of His Body. These saints have "washed their robes and made them white in the blood of the Lamb" (Rev. 7:14) and rejoice in their salvation (Rev. 7:10). They serve night and day in God's temple (Rev. 7:15) and receive the same millennial blessings as the raptured ones (Rev. 7:16-17).

A united Israel (Judah and Ephraim) will be devoted to her Messiah during His earthly reign. Her inclusion in His Body, by no means, takes away her exalted and distinctive role as head of the nations during the Millennium (Jer. 31:7, Isa 61:9). In a dream the Lord gave me on March 12, 2005, He indicated the Jewish remnant in the wilderness will become a part of His holy congregation, although she will come *very* late to this glorious position:

March 12, 2005

Destruction of the Many-Headed Beast

When the dream opened, I appeared to be the sole spectator in an empty movie theatre. I saw a silhouette of my head as I watched a drama unfold before my eyes. Yet, the entire time I felt as though I was in the scene, a part of the action.

My eyes first focused on a huge stone mountain. Without warning, the mountain began to shift and loosen. Suddenly, a gigantic beast with many heads formed; it tore away from the mountain's surface.

The colossal fiend began to chase a small wispy shadow of a figure. The ground shook as the creature chased the figure. I could not tell if the figure was a man or a woman, because it was so small compared to the multiheaded beast.

The small figure ran into the desert and then into a small cave. Each massive head of the beast snipped at the small figure as it fled into the cave. The tyrant tried to force its way into the tiny space but could not enter.

Suddenly, there was an explosion. I watched in awe as the ruthless brute was blown to bits. Debris flew in every direction until it was unrecognizable rubble on the ground!

Afterward, an old white convertible pulled up to the cave. It was filled with people. A slender woman with long black hair and attired in an all-white suit, exited the car. She also wore a big hat and a corsage pinned to her suit jacket. I knew she was Christ's bride because I heard the word "bride" spoken as she exited the car. As the woman approached the cave, the little figure came out to greet the woman. The hatted lady asked, "Are you ready to go to church now?"

The multiheaded beast in my dream represents the 10-horn dragon (10-nation, UN confederacy) under Satan's control during the Great Tribulation. It will be the last Gentile power to rule earth before Christ's return. The little, wispy shadow of a figure trying to find refuge from the beast in a desert cave, is the remnant of Jews (and others of Hebrew descent perchance) that escapes the Antichrist.

As the mammoth monster tries to destroy the remnant, Christ will destroy it at His Second Coming. This last empire—and all the vestiges of the prior ones—will be obliterated from the face of the earth. Consequently, a remnant of Jews will be saved from destruction.

During the Millennium, a united Israel will assume her rightful role as head of the nations. Jews will have accepted Christ Yeshua as their Lord and Savior. They are no different from the raptured saints who went before them, nor are they different from those who were tortured or martyred for their faith during the Great Tribulation. Everybody will acknowledge and worship Christ as their Messiah!

The Head Needs Its Whole Body

No head can function without its body, and no body can function without its head. And in a natural childbirth, the head should precede the body as the birth of the Christ Child, who became the Head of the Church, preceded His Body. Together, Christ and His Body—also called His bride—are one unit, one flesh. Christ and His Church are emblematic of this one-flesh concept, demonstrated in a husband-wife relationship. When he wrote to the Ephesian Church, the Apostle Paul connected the one-flesh idea to Christ and His bride:

> *For we are members of His body, of His flesh and of His bones. "For this reason a man shall leave his father and mother and be joined to his wife, and the two shall become one flesh." This is a great mystery, but I speak concerning Christ and the church (Eph. 5:30-32).*

Christ, our Head, cannot usher in His reign of righteousness on earth without His Church (Body). This means His *whole* Body, including the little remnant in the desert. His entire Body (bride) will be fully, completely delivered at His Second Coming. Once the whole Body of Christ is delivered, she can rule the nations with Him as a chaste bride.

Thus, all of creation awaits Israel's cry in the wilderness for her Messiah. She is the one at age's end who will marshal in His return. She must come to a complete and utter end of herself and of her reliance on everything that is not God:

> *Then I heard the man clothed in linen, who was above the waters of the river, when he held up his right hand and his left hand to heaven, and swore by Him who lives forever, that it shall be for a time, times, and half time; and when the power of the holy people has been completely shattered, all these things shall be finished (Dan. 12:7).*

"And it shall be in that day," says the Lord, "that I will cut off your horses from your midst and destroy your chariots. I will cut off the cities of your land and throw down all your strongholds. I will cut off sorceries from your hand, and you shall have no soothsayers. Your carved images, I will also cut off, and your sacred pillars from your midst. You shall no more worship the work of your hands; I will pluck your wooden images from your midst. Thus, I will destroy your cities. And I will execute vengeance in anger and fury on the nations that have not heard" (Mi. 5:10-15).

Until Israel becomes that desperate, repentant woman in the wilderness who delivers Messiah to a broken planet, all creation labors in the throes of birth pangs:

For the earnest expectation of the creation eagerly waits for the revealing of the sons of God. For the creation was subjected to futility, not willingly, but because of Him who subjected it in hope; because the creation itself also will be delivered from the bondage of corruption …. For we know that the whole creation groans and labors with birth pangs together until now (Rom. 8:20-22).

Chapter Seven
The Great Tribulation

A discussion of the Great Tribulation is in order here. At its beginning, the Antichrist is unveiled to the world. Sometime shortly before or afterward, the *second* male child is born. He will be caught up to God's throne, and a remnant of Israel will flee to the wilderness (Rev. 12:5b-6, 13:5). The Great Tribulation is the last three and a half years of this present age. The Antichrist will ruthlessly rule the planet. It will be a horrific time of suffering for Israel, Christian believers, and the world.

The Great Tribulation is the last half—three and a half years—of Daniel's 70th week. Daniel's 70th week is the final seven-year period of 70 "weeks" or 490 years that ends with sin's final judgment and Christ's reign of righteousness. The Church widely teaches 483 of the 490 years of Gabriel's prophecy to Daniel have been fulfilled and seven years remain to be fulfilled. However, it is the author's belief that 486½ of the 490 years have already come to pass. Only three and a half years remain to be fulfilled, and we are right on the cusp of the Antichrist's worldwide unveiling! (Refer to Chart on page 56.)

Gabriel, speaking to Daniel about his people, declared:

Seventy weeks are determined for your people and for your holy city, to finish the transgression, to make an end of sins, to make reconciliation for iniquity, to bring in everlasting righteousness, to seal up the vision and prophecy, and to anoint the Most Holy (Dan. 9:24).

The first three goals—to finish the transgression, make an end of sins, make reconciliation for iniquity—were fulfilled at Christ's First Advent. The last three goals—to bring in everlasting righteousness, seal up the vision and prophecy, and anoint the Most Holy—will be completed at Christ's Second Advent. Christ's public ministry as the Suffering-Servant Savior (First Advent) lasted exactly three and a half years. At that time, His sacrifice as the perfect Lamb of God "put an end to all sacrifice and offering." He was "cut off" as was the old sacrificial system.

The last three and a half years of that "holy week" is the Great Tribulation, the time of Jacob's trouble. It leads to Christ's return as the Conquering Judge and King of kings. He will pour out His wrath on the nations under Satan's sway as they seek to destroy Israel.

DANIEL'S 70th WEEK – A HOLY WEEK
(Final 7 years of Gabriel's Prophecy to Daniel)

Christ 's First Advent	Christ's Second Advent
Earthly ministry lasted three and a half years	Great Tribulation will last three and a half years
Christ came as a Suffering Servant	Christ returns as a Conquering Judge and King
Purpose:	**Purpose:**
Finish the transgression	Bring in everlasting righteousness
Make an end of sins	Seal up vision and prophecy
Make reconciliation for iniquity	Anoint the Most Holy (as Ruler of earth)

The Church's confusion about whether we are dealing with a remaining seven years or three and a half years lies in a verse from the same prophecy Gabriel gave Daniel:

> *Then he shall confirm a covenant with many for one week; but in the middle of the week he shall bring an end to sacrifice and offering. And on the wing of abominations shall be one who makes desolate, even until the consummation which is determined, is poured out on the desolate (Dan. 9:27).*

The key lies in identifying who "he" is in the verse. Who confirms a covenant with many for one week and brings an end to sacrifice and offering? Many Bible teachers identify "he" as the Antichrist. They believe the "son of perdition" will break a seven-year peace treaty ("covenant") with Israel at the three-and-a-half-year-mark. At that time, the man of iniquity will set up the "abomination of desolation" in Israel's temple, cutting off all Jewish sacrifices and offerings.

The Syrian ruler, Antiochus IV Epiphanes, who foreshadowed the Antichrist, halted all worship and banned the daily sacrifices in his day (167-168 B.C.). He even sacrificed a pig on the altar and erected a statue in Israel's temple in honor of Zeus. This was the abomination of desolation spoken of in Daniel 11:31 and Daniel 12:11.

Scripture reveals that the Antichrist will also set up an "abomination of desolation" in a holy place (Matt. 24:15). Surely, this will stop all worship of God there. However, I am fully convinced the Church should *not* be looking for the Antichrist to renege on a seven-year treaty ("covenant") with Israel at its midpoint. The Church waits for a false sign if she is waiting for a covenant to be signed and broken.

An alternative interpretation of Daniel 9:27 is: He (Christ) shall confirm a covenant with many for one week (seven years), but in the middle of the week or after three and a half years, He shall bring an end to sacrifice and offering. In this interpretation, "he" refers to Christ, not the Antichrist.

The Masoretic Text, which is the most ancient, offers this translation: *"And one week shall confirm the covenant to many, and in the middle of the week My sacrifice and offering shall be taken away."* During Christ's First Advent, His once-and-for-all sacrifice as the perfect Lamb of God ended all sacrifices and offerings under the Old Testament Law. Daniel 9:27 refers to this!

Furthermore, the Hebrew word for covenant ("bereeth" or "berith") used in Daniel 9:27 signifies a *divine* agreement or pledge—a promise made between God and His people. Christ made such a covenant at the Last Supper:

> *And as they were eating, Jesus took the bread, blessed and broke it, and gave it to His disciples and said, "Take, eat; this is My body." Then He took the cup, and gave thanks, and gave it to them, saying, "Drink from it, all of you. For this is My blood of the new covenant, which is shed for many for the remission of sins (Matt. 26:26-28, emphasis mine).*

The institution of the Lord's Supper occurred during the last week of Christ's earthly ministry, in Daniel's 70th week! Three and a half years into that 70th week, Christ was cut off—not for Himself, but for others. His shed blood confirmed a promised covenant (Rom. 15:8).

God's Word teaches Christ is a Covenant Promise to the people. He is the Mediator of a better covenant than the one under Moses:

I, the Lord, have called You in righteousness, and will hold Your hand; I will keep You and give You as a covenant to the people, as a light to the Gentiles, *to open blind eyes, to bring prisoners from the prison, those who sit in darkness from the prison house* (Is. 42:6-7, emphasis mine).

In an acceptable time I have heard You, in the day of salvation I have helped You; I will preserve You and give You as a covenant to the people, to restore the earth, to cause them to inherit the desolate heritages; *that You may say to the prisoners, "Go forth," to those who are in darkness, "Show yourselves"....* (Is. 49:8-9, emphasis mine).

But now He has obtained a more excellent ministry, inasmuch as He is also Mediator for a better covenant which was established on better promises. *For if that first covenant had been faultless, then no place would have been sought for a second. ...In that* He says, 'A new covenant,' He has made the first obsolete. *Now what is becoming obsolete and growing old is ready to vanish away* (Heb. 8:6-7, 13, emphasis mine).

Behold, the days are coming, says the Lord, when I will make a new covenant with the house of Israel and with the house of Judah—*not according to the covenant that I made with their fathers in the day that I took them by the hand to lead them out of the land of Egypt, My covenant which they broke, though I was a husband to them, says the Lord.* But this is the covenant that I will make with the house of Israel after those days, says the Lord: *I will put My law in their minds, and write it on their hearts; and I will be their God, and they shall be My people* (Jer. 31:31-33, emphasis mine).

As a final point, the phrasing in Daniel 9:27 in the New King James, New American Standard, English Standard, and others suggests the one who "confirms a covenant with many" is different from the one who "makes desolate" (Antichrist). After speaking of he who confirms a seven-year covenant with many, the verse continues:

And on the wing of abominations shall be one who makes desolate, even until the consummation which is determined, is poured out on the desolate (Dan. 9:27b, emphasis mine, New American Standard Bible).

The usage of "And" and "shall be one" suggests the one who confirms a covenant and the one who makes desolate are two different persons. In the first half of Daniel 9:27, the person is referred to as "he." But in the second half of the same verse, it says there "shall be one," which gives the impression someone else is being introduced, the desolator.

If the first half of Daniel's 70ᵗʰ week (3½ years) was completed at Christ's First Coming, then the Church should not be looking for a seven-year peace treaty ("covenant") to be signed and broken by the Antichrist at midpoint! According to Christ's discourse on the Mount of Olives, the Great Tribulation will commence as soon as Jews see the "abomination of desolation standing in the holy place" (Matt. 24:15-22).

It is worth noting, some scholars argue that this "abomination" was fulfilled in 70 A.D., when the Roman General Titus and his army overthrew Jerusalem and massacred hundreds of thousands of Jews. Before plundering and burning the city to the ground, they made many abominable sacrifices to their gods in the holy temple.

However, the destruction of Jerusalem and its temple in 70 A.D. does not *fully* fulfill these words spoken in Christ's Olivet Discourse:

For then there will be great tribulation such as has not been since the beginning of the world until this time, no, nor ever shall be. And until those days were shortened, no flesh would be saved; but for the elect's sake those days will be shortened (Matt. 24:21-22).

The "holy place" Christ spoke of in Matthew 24:15 refers to the temple, where Jews make sacrifices and offerings. However, as of this typing, the Third Temple—to be erected on the sacred Temple Mount, where Solomon and Herod's temples were built—is presently controlled by Muslims. Technically, "the holy place" does not yet exist. Nevertheless, devout Jews in the Holy Land have been preparing for its supernatural erection for many years.

If you have read my books, *Two Hidden Treasures* or *The Late Great United States*, then you know I contend that the 44th President of the United States of America, Barack Hussein Obama, is the future Antichrist. I am fully persuaded he is the "little horn" that will rise out of a "10-horn" United Nations confederacy during that last three and a half years of this age. In *The Late Great United States*, I devote three chapters explaining why Barack Obama is the forthcoming "son of perdition." My grounds for this assertion cannot be adequately recapped in this book.

None of this may not be as far-fetched as it seems.

On April 10, 2013, the Lord gave me a dream, in which Obama suffered a mortal head wound and revived! In the dream, he suddenly disappeared, and a sinister man-beast appeared in his place. The beast resembled an animal *and* a man. And it was clear he was a beast of war. He would shed much blood.

April 10, 2013

A Dream: Obama's Head Wound and the Beast

It is now 5:54 in the morning. I just woke up from a dream. In the dream, I found myself standing on something to look up and out of an old warehouse window. I was in the middle of nowhere. Lots of open land surrounded the warehouse; there were also a few small one-room wooden structures in the distance.

Suddenly, I saw men in dark blue windbreakers. They were standing near the warehouse but facing away from it. The words ATF came to my spirit, although I never saw the words on the back of their jackets. I saw one agent smoking a cigarette. Then something happened.

I looked toward a long dirt trail, a short distance away. I saw Obama. He was dressed in a grey suit and white shirt. He had been shot in the head! Two men in dark blue windbreakers were on either side of him, holding him up. A white bandage had been wrapped around his head. It was bloodied from the wound.

Suddenly, a furry growling THING appeared where Obama had been! Obama was gone. The THING was covered completely in brown fur, like a bear, but it walked upright like a man and it growled things to people and itself. It had a long assault weapon in its hand. The thing was a beast of war.

At first, its back was to me. Then, it slowly turned around. I saw its face. It had the face of an animal with dark black circles for eyes, yet it appeared to be a man.

It looked directly at me through the little window in the warehouse, which seemed impossible since the window was so small and high up. The beast knew I was in the warehouse, peering at it! An overwhelming terror struck my heart. "It's here! It's here!" I kept whispering to myself.

In Revelation 13, a multiheaded beast rises out of the sea. This beast represents the Antichrist's empire emerging from the abyss. One of its many heads suffers a fatal head wound! But it is miraculously healed:

And I saw one of his heads as if it had been mortally wounded, and his deadly wound was healed. And all the world marveled and followed the beast. So they worshipped the dragon who gave authority to the beast; and they worshipped the beast saying,

"Who is like the beast? Who is able to make war with him?" (Rev. 13:3-4).

It appears Barack Obama will suffer a head wound sometime during his political career. U.S. Alcohol, Tobacco and Firearm (ATF) agents will be around or involved when he is shot. The wound will prove fatal. However, because Obama disappeared and, in his place, stood the beast—the Antichrist—Satan will incarnate his body. Satan will make it appear as if the wound was not fatal. From that point on, the United States and the world will be dealing with Satan himself. The assault rifle in the hand of the beast indicates the Antichrist will promote conflict and war. Woe to the earth!

The Antichrist's Unveiling and the Rapture

Will the Church be raptured *before* the Antichrist is unveiled? For a myriad of reasons, she may not. But I will discuss only three.

First, tens of thousands of people by now suspect Barack Obama is the future Antichrist. Thousands *know* he is. Technically, he is already unveiled! Those of us who know who he is are just waiting for the rest of Church (and world) to wake up!

Second, the rapture is patterned after the Great Exodus of Moses' time. We can expect an expression of that celebrated event to be repeated under the New Covenant of Christ. (See Chapter 12 for a fuller discussion on God's use of shadows, patterns, and types to communicate coming events.) When God smote Egypt with all His wonders, it was not until the fourth plague that He made a distinction between the children of Israel, who lived in Goshen, and the Egyptians. God allowed the first three plagues—a blood-tainted Nile River, a lice infestation, and a frog invasion—to touch the lives of His people. But starting with the fourth plague—swarms of flies—God made the following distinction:

> *And in that day I will set apart the land of Goshen, in which My people dwell, that no swarms of flies shall be there, in order that you may know that I am the Lord in the midst of the land. I will make a difference between My people and your people (Ex. 8:22-23a).*

Third, and most importantly, the Lord is returning for a chaste bride, one without spot, blemish, or wrinkle (Eph. 5:26-27, 2 Cor. 11:2). He has given me numerous dreams that indicate His Church, for the most part, walks lockstep with the fallen cultures of the world and not according to His Word. She is asleep and needs to be awakened.

He has also given me multiple dreams in which His bride, at last, awakes! At that point, she is finally fully conscious of the fallen state of the world around her and has detached from it. But she arrives at this awakened state only after a time of intense trial.

In these latter dreams, she is so wakeful and alert that her huge eyes overshadow the rest of her face. The wide eyes are symbolic of her new enlightenment. Likewise, in many of these dreams, she is attired in white or in a white wedding gown. In the previous dreams, she wore black, stripes, or other patterns. Most encouraging of all is there are no signs of self-indulgence in the latter dreams. For example, she is no longer obese, living in extravagant homes, surrounded by lush trappings, or indulging in oversized food portions. She is focused on Christ alone. The Lord is returning for a chaste bride. The Body must match the Head.

The Lord will cleanse and refine His spotted bride before taking her home to be with Him. At a set time on God's calendar, during the Great Tribulation, the Lord will remove His bride. In 1 Corinthians 15:52, the Apostle Paul reveals a mystery about the rapture: "*In a moment, in the twinkling of an eye,* at the last trump*: for the trumpet shall sound, and the dead shall be raised incorruptible, and we shall be changed.*" (emphasis mine). Could the rapture be *after* the seventh and final trumpet judgment ("last trump"), but *before* the seven bowl judgments?

God's full wrath is poured out on the nations during the final seven bowl judgments. The Lord's bride is not appointed to wrath (1 Thess. 5:9). Yet, if the rapture occurs just *before* the seven bowl judgments, the Lord's bride will have undergone a period of intense trial. Free of dross and bonds, she will be spotless and ready for her Bridegroom. Should the Lord return before that cleansing-refining period, only a few would go.

The Lord called me to be a "sign of the bride to come." He used my life as a literal sign to help members of His corporate bride catch sight of their shameful spots and blemishes. At times, many of us fail to discern in ourselves wrong beliefs and patterns of thinking that lead to injurious, detrimental behaviors. Yet we easily see these faults in others. It is God's intent that His bride see herself in me, to see how I used to be before He refined me by trial and fire.

God made me a sign for another equally important reason. He desires to assure His beloved that she will be caught up to heaven in the same manner Joshua and I will have been caught up. We will go before her as a sign that she, too, will soon follow. At that point, the world will have so unraveled, she will need the reassurance.

DANIEL'S SEVENTY WEEKS

(490 years decreed for Israel's Final Deliverance/Daniel 9)

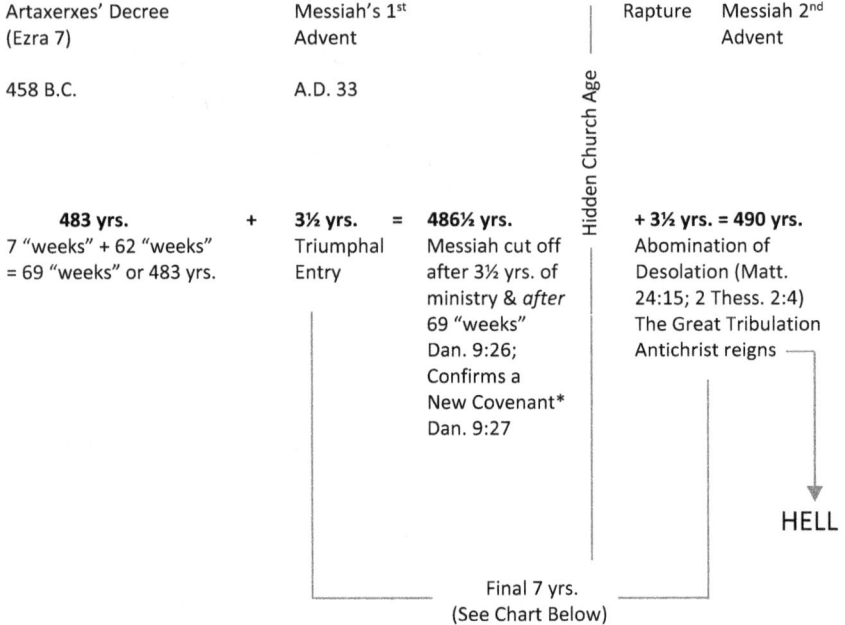

Artaxerxes' Decree
(Ezra 7)

Messiah's 1st
Advent

Rapture   Messiah 2nd
Advent

458 B.C.

A.D. 33

Hidden Church Age

483 yrs.   +   **3½ yrs.**   =   **486½ yrs.**   **+ 3½ yrs. = 490 yrs.**
7 "weeks" + 62 "weeks"   Triumphal   Messiah cut off   Abomination of
= 69 "weeks" or 483 yrs.   Entry   after 3½ yrs. of   Desolation (Matt.
                                           ministry & *after*   24:15; 2 Thess. 2:4)
                                           69 "weeks"   The Great Tribulation
                                           Dan. 9:26;   Antichrist reigns
                                           Confirms a
                                           New Covenant*
                                           Dan. 9:27

HELL

Final 7 yrs.
(See Chart Below)

*Instituted at The Last Supper

Daniels' 70th Week
A Holy Week (Final 7 years of Gabriel's Prophecy to Daniel)

CHRIST'S FIRST ADVENT	CHRIST'S SECOND ADVENT
Earthly ministry lasted 3½ years	The Great Tribulation will last 3½ years
Christ as Suffering Servant	Christ as Conquering Judge and King
PURPOSE:	PURPOSE:
Finish the transgression	Bring in everlasting righteousness
Make an end of sins	Seal up vision and prophecy
Make reconciliation for iniquity	Anoint the Most Holy

Chapter Eight
Dreaming about Joshua and Our Snatching Up

In the spring of 1998, the Lord began to disclose more to me about Joshua by way of dreams. He did this through my dreams and through the dreams of others. One of the most revealing dreams about the birth of Joshua was given to a friend of mine, who relayed it to me.

April 18, 1998

A Friend's Dream: A Special Baby Boy is Born

My friend called today to tell me about an extraordinary dream she dreamt on April 17. She asked God to wipe the dream from her memory if it was not from Him—to not remember it in the morning. She remembered every detail.

In the dream, four of us were at a restaurant having dinner—she, her husband, my husband, and me. I was pregnant, but I did not look pregnant. Suddenly, my water broke. She and I excused ourselves from the table. We gathered cloth napkins and made our way to the bathroom.

I went into a "painless labor" as soon as we entered the bathroom. I experienced no discomfort. She prayed fervently to God to allow her to see the baby. If it fell to her to deliver the child, she wanted him to be visible. For fear she might be struck dead, she also prayed to know if she should touch the baby.

Suddenly, two angels appeared. They told her they would take over. I delivered a radiant, translucent baby boy with shocking white hair and blue eyes. She placed a white cloth on the top of his head and kissed it. Afterward, the four of us disappeared. She exited the bathroom alone.

Her husband was stunned when he saw her. "What happened to you?" he asked. Her hair—naturally blonde—was now snow white. Also, her face had a luminous glow!

"I was in the presence of God," she said.

When I began to dissect Revelation 12:1-6, this dream revealed critical information to me. At first glance, the dream seemed to contradict the text. The woman in Revelation 12 cries out in pain to deliver her child. But in the dream, I have a painless labor. Further, after giving birth the woman flees into the wilderness. Only the child is caught up to God's throne. In the dream, both Joshua and I are taken.

As mentioned earlier, it took me years to discover the Scripture passage is layered. Understanding the multiple layers dispels all ambiguity. Some verses refer to Israel, the nation (vv. 1, 6). One verse applies to Mary and Christ (v. 5a). Other verses relate to the second woman and the second child (vv. 2, 4, 5b). Both women symbolize Israel, but at different points in history.

The painful labor in the passage is symbolic of the agony Israel will experience during the three-and-a-half-year reign of the Antichrist. After that, a remnant of Jews (and possibly others of Hebrew descent) will finally "deliver" Christ to an almost decimated world. But this will require her brokenness and repentance. Thus, she is the "woman" who flees into the wilderness, to a place prepared for her by God. In that place, she is nurtured and preserved by Him. During this process, she is finally brought to a place of regret, remorse, and repentance.

On the other hand, I will be caught up with Joshua just before those three and a half years as a "sign of the bride to come." I am a sign to Christ's corporate bride that she, too, will be taken to heaven before Christ pours out His wrath on the rebellious nations of the world.

Some may ask how I can be so sure that I will be taken with Joshua. How can I trust my friend's dream? The Lord always establishes a matter with at least two witnesses (Deut. 17:6, 19:15, John 8:17). Thus, two weeks after my friend relayed the dream about Joshua's birth to me, God gave her another.

Her second dream was longer and much more elaborate. It had to be to serve the purpose God needed it to serve. At first, I did not understand its meaning or significance. Then, I lived it! Moreover, what happened in the dream unfolded in real life on the exact date the Lord revealed in the dream.

In my friend's dream, I tried three times to catch a plane to Miami. But each time, I was thwarted. Six weeks after her dream, I was invited to attend a business conference in Miami. Three times during that trip I had to abandon a hotel for the same three reasons I could not board a plane in my friend's dream.

Below are two journal excerpts I present for your examination. The first entry reveals the dream. The second excerpt discusses its amazing fulfillment.

May 9, 1998

My Friend's Dream: My Trip to Miami

My friend called me to relay, yet another strange dream she had about me. She had been trying to take an afternoon nap. Her voicemail message to me said, "Obviously, God is not going to let me sleep until I tell you this dream. It happened a week ago. I should have told you then."

Following is the dream she relayed to me:

You were pregnant. You wore a red business suit. You were in an airport, trying to catch a flight home. But you were not trying to catch a flight to Greenville-Spartanburg. For some reason, you were trying to get home to Miami.

Your flight was oversold. You went from airline to airline, trying to get a flight home, only to discover a problem with each plane. You tried three times. However, not being able to fly turned out to be a big blessing for you.

The first airplane had to return because it was losing fuel. They had to ground the plane. On the second airplane, all the passengers thought they were going to Miami, but the pilot took them to a different destination. The third airplane had to make an emergency landing in the middle of nowhere after one of its engines blew out.

The next scene reminded me of the film, Home Alone. *The mother tried to get back to her young son, who had been inadvertently left at home when the family traveled to Paris for the Christmas holiday. She had the hardest time trying to catch a flight home. Near the end of the film, she's riding in a truck with a group of musicians.*

In my dream, you were riding in the front of a truck, surrounded by musicians. The inside of the vehicle was so bright! The musicians were all radiant and glowing. They appeared to be angels. You were dressed in gold. You were so happy, so thrilled. Then, I woke up.

Before my friend finished her voicemail, she said: "Oh yeah, for some reason, June 12 sticks out in my mind."

Approximately six weeks later, I recorded the following journal entry:

June 14, 1998

A Dream Come True!

On May 9, 1998, my friend relayed a strange dream to me by voicemail. She dreamt it a week prior to telling me. The day she told me she had been trying to nap. But she soon realized God was not going to let her sleep until she shared the dream.

In the dream, I was trying to get home to Miami, Florida, not Greenville-Spartanburg, the region of South Carolina, where I live. My flight was oversold. The fact that I wore a red business suit suggests I was traveling on business.

I had a difficult time trying to fly home. I tried three times. Three times I was blocked. But this worked to my advantage. In the end, I was surrounded by angels, and I was dressed in gold. The last thing she said was June 12 stuck out in her mind.

No Room at the Inn

Little did I know when my friend dreamt this dream six weeks ago, I would take a business trip to Miami. I had no trouble getting there. I flew in on Denny's private jet.

Due to a strange series of circumstances, however, I lost my hotel room after only one night's stay. Claudia, my executive assistant, booked me for two nights, but the hotel did not have the second night's reservation. I should have discovered the mistake when I checked in, but at the time there was a big mix-up with the reservations of several other guests. Some were irate. The check-in clerk was completely distracted with that debacle at the time of my check in. And I failed to catch the error myself.

At dawn, I discovered the bill underneath my door. I called the front desk for an explanation. There was nothing the hotel could do. It was sold out. Unless the manager could find me another room, which appeared doubtful, I needed to check out by noon.

As I waited to hear back from the hotel manager, I decided I should try to find another hotel. Did I really want to stay another night where I was? So far, it had not been a pleasant experience.

The hotel was extremely expensive and considered a landmark. But its accommodations were atrocious. The building had once been a hospital. Converted now into a hotel, it was old, rickety, and very noisy. In fact, hallway noises kept waking me during the night.

I decided to move to another hotel, nearby. I would transfer to the one where several of the conference events had been moved. That, too, had been a strange turn of events. At first, the entire business conference was to take place at the hotel where I was. However, a day before the event, we were informed some conference activities would be moved to another hotel. The conference officials distributed flyers explaining the sudden change. They arranged for a shuttle service between the two hotels since the change of venue created a major inconvenience for the meeting participants.

I decided to call the second hotel to make a reservation. A woman answered the phone. I was told the reservation clerk was not in. Then, "Hold Please!" I waited and waited ... and waited for the woman to return. After a while, I decided the extended hold was not a good sign. I sensed I would probably receive more poor service for another extravagant price. I hung up.

Until I was settled somewhere, however, I could not concentrate on the conference. Suddenly, I had an idea. I decided to move to a much cheaper hotel on the other side of town. I stayed at that hotel many times before. It was out of the way, several miles from the conference, but at least it was an excellent value for the money. Besides, I had a rental car to get back and forth. And I could leave my bags in the car until I checked into the hotel. This was an emergency. I had to compromise. I called Claudia to make the reservation. Within minutes, she called me back with a reservation number.

A Wonderful Evening with Friends

On the last day of the conference, I planned to spend the evening with Jeri and return to my hotel. She and her family reside in South Miami. After the conference, I went straight to her house. I had not seen her or her girls in such a long time. I missed them desperately. I could hardly wait to get there.

At her house, I changed into casual clothes. I had been there only 10 minutes when Jeri decided I should spend the night at her house. She was adamant. I was reluctant to call the hotel because I knew it was too late to cancel the reservation. Nevertheless, Jeri insisted. Reluctantly, I call the hotel manager. I explained my situation and asked not to be charged as a no-show. Much to my surprise, he cancelled my reservation without charge. So, I was free to spend the night with Jeri and her family.

After a scrumptious dinner, I changed into my gold silk nightgown. Jeri and I talked, laughed, joked, and mused over countless recollections. We even sang songs. We talked and reminisced for 11 straight hours! At 5 a.m., after only one hour's sleep, I got up, got dressed, and headed for the airport. I could not remember having so much fun.

Real Life Parallels

As I was flying home, the parallels between my friend's dream and what happened to me on that trip began to dawn on me. First, I am pregnant (in the Spirit), but only a handful of people know this. Second, I was on a business trip. Third, the event took place in Miami. Fourth, I found myself in a sold-out situation. Fifth, that predicament resulted in my searching for accommodations at three different hotels.

Interestingly, the first hotel just could not deliver the service. This was much like the airline in my friend's dream that was grounded because of no fuel. It could not get the job done.

The second hotel happened to be a surprise to all the conference attendees. Originally, we thought the hotel where we were staying was where the entire conference would take place. The change of venue was an unexpected inconvenience for many of us. Was this not like the second airline in my friend's dream? In that instance, people thought they were going one place, but ended up somewhere else.

The third hotel I picked was an emergency choice. It was located on the other side of town, but it was a reasonable value. This was like the third airline in my friend's dream that had to make an emergency stop in the middle of nowhere.

Further,

- *After all the snags, I ended up spending the night with my best friend, whom I had not seen in a long time. ("Not being able to fly turned out to be a big blessing for you.")*
- *Spending time with Jeri and her family was like being at home. ("For some reason you were trying to get home to Miami.")*
- *Surrounded by people I loved; I had a ball. ("You were so happy, so thrilled.")*
- *I slept in a gold nightgown, albeit for one hour. ("You were dressed in gold.")*
- *Jeri and I sang songs. ("You were surrounded by musicians.")*
- *Surely, the events of that trip were the handiwork of angels.*

Finally, I remembered one last aspect of my friend's dream. I frantically searched my briefcase for my boarding pass. I wanted to check the date. Not having slept for nearly a day, I had lost all track of time. The date on my boarding pass: JUNE 12!

As I waited for the last leg of my flight, I pondered the significance of the dream. Why did the Lord give my friend such an involved dream and then have me fulfill it six weeks later? Everything He does has a purpose. Certainly, He was not making a commentary on the state of hotels in Miami. So, what was the importance of her dream and my having to live that chronicle of events? Instantly, the answer came to me.

God was making a crucial point. If my friend's second dream could unfold with such real-life precision, then I could also trust her first dream about me. In her first dream, I gave birth to Joshua. Afterward, both of us were taken to heaven by two angels.

As it turned out, the second dream was as essential as the first. It sealed in my heart that I would accompany my child to heaven when he is snatched up to God's throne. I am not the woman in Revelation 12 who flees into the wilderness to be fed and nurtured by God for 1,260 days. That's another "woman." She is a Jewish remnant that also symbolizes Israel in the passage.

Chapter Nine
Ordinary, Yet Special

The Lord has given me glimpses of Joshua's personality in numerous dreams. In many way, he appears to be ordinary, yet special. He is all boy and frequently gets into childish dilemmas. But in later dreams, he is not the least bit rambunctious. When presented as a young man, he seems particularly courteous and gallant. I am now reminded of a dream the Lord gave Jeri's friend Robin, who I never had the pleasure of meeting. She knew of me through Jeri. One day, Robin called Jeri to relate a dream she had about me.

"Does Ray have a son?" she asked.

"Girl, I did not know where she was going with this," Jeri recounted to me later. "I froze. I didn't know what to say. Finally, I said, 'No, she has a daughter named Ryan.'"

"No, she has a son," Robin insisted. "I saw him in a dream. He was a maître d' on a large ship. He was a young man and extremely courteous. A white napkin was draped across his arm as he served the people. Many people asked him for things. He was so polite. He appeared to be a young man of color, only with pale skin," she said.

I was not at all surprised that Joshua, as a young man, would be portrayed as a well-mannered servant of the people. Look at his

Dad. How could he not be? But I confess I was taken aback by Robin's physical description of him. That was not the first time he had been described as pale. Some had described him as "almost white." (We will address the issue of race in Chapter 14, the last chapter of this book.)

In one of my very first dreams about Joshua, the Lord revealed how life might be for him, at least at first:

April 29, 1998

A Dream: An Ordinary, Yet Special Child

In my second dream of the night, I saw a group of little children with their adult chaperons. They were walking in a snowy meadow. They were on a field trip. Suddenly, I noticed three little boys walking behind a man. They were all the same age, no more than four years old. Seconds earlier, they had been with a larger group, but for some reason, the Lord separated these three in a single frame.

The little trio toddled behind the man like ducks. They could not keep their balance and kept falling. Tumbling in the snow, they were having the time of their lives. Although there was snow everywhere, they were oblivious to the cold. Their jackets were open.

"Which one got his head stuck between the stair railings?" someone asked.

"My son—the one with the pink hair," I responded very matter-of-factly. At that moment, I saw the middle boy had shocking pink hair. Not only that, but a stalk of it also sprouted from the crown of his head; it had been gathered in a rubber band.

The other two lads appeared like regular four-year-old boys. Although Joshua fit right in with the two youngsters in every way, his pink hair signaled he was different. But no one treated him differently. Moreover, he seemed to be totally unaware that he was a little odd.

From the very beginning, the Lord indicated Joshua would be a challenge for me. In one dream, he mischievously feigns sleep. He is an infant. He lies in bed peacefully with his eyes closed. After a short while he opens a single eye to see if I am watching him.

In another dream, I chase him through a crowded airport. He is a toddler weaving in and out of places and between people's legs. I cannot catch him. In still another dream, every time I glance at the backseat of the car, I discover he has unbuckled his car seat and he is standing at the window, staring out. He is just a tot. I am completely flummoxed. *How does he keep doing this?* I wonder.

In a later dream, I am in a busy department store. I am riding the up escalator. Suddenly, I see a roguish boy of about 7- or 8-years old grinning at me. He's riding the adjacent escalator, down. He's also on his knees facing backwards. His packages are sprawled on the escalator stair a few feet in front of him.

"People ought to pay more attention to their children, especially in public places," I mumble to myself. Then I realize it's Joshua! I race up the escalator. I push pass people to try to catch him.

In one of my favorite early dreams of Joshua, we are at a festive family gathering. Everyone is talking, eating, and enjoying themselves. I am in a corner, reclining on a lounger with a plate of food in my hand. Joshua appears to be a busy three-year-old. He is nattily dressed in a pair of jeans and a dark purple sweater with a starched white shirt underneath. The scene is framed in such a way that I never see his full face.

He persists in trying to climb into my lap. I keep pushing him to the floor because I am trying to finish my meal. He will not have it. He continues trying until he manages to climb up. Then he rests his little head on my chest.

At this point, I discover his mouth is overflowing with saltine crackers. It is so full I am frightened he will choke. I hold my cupped hand beneath his chin and instruct him to spit. He obeys. Two AA batteries come tumbling out of his mouth soaked in cracker crumbs. I yell, "BOY!"

"Ishi, I thought You said he was smart!" I say to Yeshua immediately upon waking.

"He *is* smart," He laughed. "But he's just a child, Ray."

This dream and others furnished me with intriguing information about Joshua at different life stages. But they also do something else. They give me a marvelous glimpse into how life will be *after* this present dispensation.

Because of Joshua's age, some of the settings cannot be earthly ones. Most likely, some are heavenly scenes. In them, I am often surrounded by loved ones. My parents, who have passed away, are present. I have also seen my siblings, other family members, and friends. Everyone appears more youthful and more attractive than I have ever known them to be. The dreams simply confirm what we as believers already know. There is a wonderful life awaiting us after this one!

Before these dreams, I never really considered how the things we enjoy in our present lives will continue into the next. In the dreams, I enjoy being in the company of dear family and friends, doing many things we do now. Also, we enjoy food—lots of it.

The Lord used the amusing dream below to convey additional information about Joshua's personality and lineage:

November 20, 2002

A Dream: My Little Striped Pony

This morning I had the most intriguing dream. In the dream, I awoke to find myself in a large bed. I turned to my right to discover a brightly colored pony standing by my bed; it was busily ripping through clothes and throwing things around the room from a large shopping bag. I took the bag from its mouth and placed it on the floor on the other side of the bed.

After I took the bag, the yellow-and-purple-striped pony shifted its attention to me. It moved closer to the head of the bed. I knew what was coming before it happened. The wild colt jumped in the bed! It nestled its large head in a pillow just underneath my arm. It was so affectionate and, at first, seemed content to lie near me. It rested horizontally at the top of the bed.

Two minutes later, it readjusted its position. In the process of making more room for its hind legs, the little pony knocked everything off the nightstand next to the bed. In the end, part of its body was on the bed and its hindquarters rested on the nightstand.

Seconds later, it was up again. Now it was like a hungry steed. Out of nowhere, a large plate of scrambled eggs and biscuits appeared in my hand. I started to feed it. With just two bites, the charger gobbled up a biscuit.

Suddenly, the little pony transformed into the cutest baby boy. He was about two years old. He was light in complexion with curly hair. The tike was dressed in white underpants and a white t-shirt that exposed a part of his little belly.

Now with his mouth wide open, the child stood on the bed at the head. I could not feed him fast enough. Without warning, he started to pick the scrambled eggs off the plate and stuff them in his mouth. He wanted to feed himself.

I told him not to touch the bed with his soiled hands. I demonstrated to him how he was not to touch the bed. Right after I finished explaining, he tripped on the bedcovers and smeared egg all over the headboard. The dream ended.

It's Joshua!

Clearly, the little striped pony symbolized Joshua. The moment I awoke, I blurted: "Oh, my goodness, he's just like me!" He was filled with unbridled energy that needed to be harnessed.

For years, Yeshua has likened me to a "wild horse" that races ahead of Him. He has told me on many occasions that before He could use me effectively in His kingdom, I needed to be reined in, restrained, and trained. Discipline was vital. Without it, I would never fulfill my call.

The high-spirited pony—ripping at clothes, jumping in the bed, knocking over things, gobbling food faster than I can feed him— represents a miniature version of me! At the same time, Joshua will be a colorful blend of the two of us as demonstrated by his bright purple and yellow stripes.

Yeshua and I have discussed this color combination on several occasions. He represents purple. I represent yellow. Purple is the color of royalty. Yellow is the color of the sun or sunshine. Not only have people called me Sunshine, the Lord sometimes uses my nickname, Ray, as a play on words: "You are ray of sun." Or, "You are the Son's Ray."

It is important to note that the pony's stripes also served another purpose. Joshua will be a blend of two groups. He will be part Jew and part Gentile.

At the time of the dream, the Lord was teaching me about the 10 lost tribes of Israel (Ephraim) and their modern-day descendants. The Jewish part of Joshua is represented by the purple stripes. The Gentile part is represented by the yellow ones. They combine to make Joshua a type of modern-day Samaritan!

In 722 B.C., fed up with their idolatry, God scattered the Northern Kingdom of Israel (Ephraim) to the nations, using Assyrian invaders. Since Ephraim wanted so much to be like the pagan Gentiles around them rather than a guiding light, God honored their desire. He strewed them to the nations.

Now more than 2,000 years after the time of Christ, many of Ephraim's descendants are hidden within His Church (Body) throughout the world, wholly unaware of their Hebrew roots. They can be considered modern-day Samaritans because they are half Hebrew and half Gentile.

Joshua—my little striped foal—will be such a descendant. His Father is a full Jew. I am part Jew and part Gentile. This makes Joshua (and me) a fitting symbol of Christ's corporate body.

Chapter Ten
Joshua: A Gift-Offering to God

According to Old Testament Law, the firstborn male belongs to the Lord (Ex. 34:19, 20b). He is set aside as a special offering or gift, consecrated to God for His sacred purposes (Ex. 13:2, 11-16). Like his Father, Joshua appears to be a promised child—a gift to God and to God's people.

Three Old Testament Scriptures indicate that at the end of days, a special offering, gift, or present will be brought to the Lord of hosts. Isaiah prophesized a gift will come to the Lord on Mount Zion from the Ethiopian people. Zephaniah heralded the "daughter of His dispersed people" will present the Lord with a special offering at the close of the age. Lastly, according to Psalm 45, a Messianic psalm, a woman referred to as the "daughter of Tyre," shall marry God's Anointed One and at His wedding she shall bring Him a special gift.

Isaiah's Reference:

> *At that time shall a present be brought to the Lord of hosts from a people tall and polished, from a people terrible from their beginning and feared and dreaded near and far, a nation strong and victorious, whose land the rivers or great channels divide—to the place [of worship] of the Name of the Lord of hosts, to Mount Zion [in Jerusalem] (Isa. 18:7, Amplified Bible, emphasis mine).*

"The people tall and polished, from a people terrible from their beginning and feared and dreaded near and far…" refers to the people of Ethiopia. According to the Scripture, the present that will be offered to the Lord on Mount Zion at the end of days comes from them. Notably, my ancestry traces to the ancient nation of Ethiopia.

Zephaniah's Reference:

> From beyond the rivers of Cush or Ethiopia those who pray to Me, the daughter of My dispersed people, will bring and present My offering" *(Zeph. 3:10, Amplified Bible, emphasis mine).*

My family is part of Israel's Diaspora. In addition to our Ethiopian heritage, we are descendants of the tribe of Judah. In 70 A.D., the Judeans were conquered and scattered by the Romans. After a 1,200-year migration across sub-Sahara Africa to the West Coast of Africa, many people of Judean heritage were put on slave ships and taken to the New World. Moses warned the Israelites that if they were disobedient to God's commands their generations would be sold as slaves and taken to distant lands on ships:

> *And the Lord will take you back to Egypt* in ships, *by the way of which I said to you, "You shall never see it again."* And there you shall be offered for sale to your enemies as male and female slaves ….* (Deut. 28:68, emphasis mine).*

Neither during the Assyrian conquest of the Northern Kingdom of Israel (Ephraim) or the Babylonian subjugation of Judah were the Israelites ever taken on slave ships! Both conquerors shared the same land mass as Israel. Consequently, there was no need for ships. The Israelites trekked!

The enslavement of Israel's heritage that involved ships happened hundreds of centuries later during the Transatlantic

Slave Trade. This tragic calamity that lasted for more than four centuries decimated millions of God's people.

At the end of days, accordingly, "the daughter of My dispersed people" will return from this centuries-long exile. But she will not return empty-handed. She shall bring a present, a special offering to the King of kings—a son.

Psalm 45 Reference:

> "And the daughter of Tyre shall be there with a gift...." (Psalm 45:12, NIV, emphasis mine).

Psalm 45 is a Messianic psalm that describes the royal wedding of Messiah to an individual referred to as the "daughter of Tyre." The New Testament book of Hebrews refers to Psalm 45 and applies it directly to Christ (Hebrews 1:8-9). Furthermore, Christ told his disciples before His ascension, *"Everything must be fulfilled that is written about Me in the Law of Moses, the Prophets, and the Psalms" (Lk. 24:44b, emphasis mine).*

The daughter of Tyre is described in vv. 9-15. In ancient times, Tyre—the world's leading commercial city-nation—was taken captive by the twin spirits of greed and covetousness. This led to its stunning downfall. God likens the United States to ancient Tyre. And, at times, He has called me its daughter.

In spring 1997, the Lord shook me with this warning: "Beware of the spirit of Tyre, daughter of Tyre." At first, I did not understand the warning or the appellation. But when He began to reveal to me that the United States was a modern-day Tyre, I came to understand I was a type of "daughter of Tyre." As an American citizen and resident, I was susceptible to being taken captive by covetousness and greed like many of my fellow countrymen. (A fuller discussion of God referring to me as a daughter of Tyre and His equating the United States with the fated merchant city of Tyre can be found in Book Three, *The Late Great United States*.)

My Special Offering

Heretofore not mentioned, at the very onset of my wondrous journey with the Lord, He placed in my hands the Christian classic *Hinds' Feet on High Places* by Hannah Hurnard. The book was given to me by a friend who had digitized my first two handwritten journals. As a result of her work, she had the opportunity to glimpse my level of intimacy with the Lord.

As I sat in her living room, relaying the most recent news the Lord had given me—that I would be embarking on a new, but arduous journey with Him—she marveled how much it paralleled the Good Shepherd's pronouncement to Much-Afraid in Hurnard's allegorical book. At that point, she gave me the book and suggested I read it.

My journey, according to the Lord, would be with Him to the "high places." He also calls these the "treacherous heights." During this expedition, He promised I would develop the "feet of deer" or hinds' feet to traipse the mountainous regions of life with Him. Hinds' feet represent a kind of surefootedness in hazardous and dangerous situations and places. My gradual ascent—like Much-Afraid's—would be long and laborious, fraught with many dangers, distresses, and disappointments.

At the beginning of Much Afraid's journey, the Good Shepherd places a seed inside of her. Near the end of her trek, she is required to make an offering of her life before she can receive her hinds' feet. By this time, the seed planted inside her at the beginning of the journey, has blossomed and is ready for removal.

Below is a brief journal excerpt discussing my sudden awareness that both Joshua and I were offerings to the Lord. Once again, He used Hurnard's *Hinds' Feet* to help bring me to that important realization.

December 28, 1999

The Offering of Joshua

I could think of nothing else last night except Joshua being a sacred offering to the Lord and that I should reread a special section in Hurnard's Hinds' Feet on High Places. *This morning before I did anything else, I reviewed that portion of the book.*

"Much Afraid," said the Voice, "take now the promise you received when I called you to follow me to the High Places, and take the natural longing for human love which you found already growing in your heart when I planted my own love there and go up into the mountains to the place that I shall show you. Offer them there as a Burnt Offering to me."[8]

In Chapter 16, Much Afraid makes her offering to the Lord, which causes her great pain. I know my experience will mirror hers.

At the beginning of my journey with the Lord, Joshua was a promise given to me. God planted him inside me, where His Spirit had already dwelt for 13 years. Joshua is a gift to me. But more importantly, he is a gift to God. I will present him to the Lord as a special offering at the close of the age. However, getting to that place of offering the Son a son will cost me everything. Thus, I, too, am an offering.

---

[8]Hannah Hurnard, *Hinds' Feet on High Places*, Tyndale House Publishers, 1975, p. 198.

Chapter Eleven
The Prince

After I detected the bump in my tummy in March 1998, the Lord waited nearly a year and a half to tell me Joshua was the mysterious prince in Ezekiel 44-46 and 48. Until that time, I only knew he was the child who will be caught up to God's throne just before the Great Tribulation. If God had not revealed the connection between the male child in Revelation 12 (vv. 2, 4, and 5b) and the grown prince in Ezekiel, I never would have associated the two.

Some argue the mystifying prince in Ezekiel is the Messiah. However, He cannot be Yeshua. He is someone distinct from Him. First, the prince eats bread in the presence of Messiah (Eze. 44:3). Second, he worships Him (Eze. 46:2, 11-12). Furthermore, the Messiah is a Priest (Ps. 110:4, Zech. 6:12-13); the prince is not (Eze. 46:2). Most importantly, the prince has sins for which he offers sacrifice (Eze. 45:22). This mysterious person cannot be our sinless Savior and Redeemer!

Others argue the prince is King David, citing such verses as Ezekiel 37:25: *"My servant David shall be their prince forever."* However, a deeper dive into Scripture reveals another 19 references to "My servant David." They all refer to Christ Yeshua, the Davidic Prince. Christ is the biological descendant of King David. Through his line, He is destined to rule forever.

The prince is mentioned at least 14 times in Ezekiel 44-46 and 48. He is set aside and consecrated to the Lord for special service during Christ's millennial reign. According to these four chapters, while he is not a priest like his Father, he has sacred duties in leading Israel's 12 tribes in worship during the appointed feasts.

John MacArthur's commentary suggests the prince may be a chief administrator of some kind with very distinctive kingdom responsibilities:

> Most likely "the prince" is one who is neither a priest nor the king, but rather one who administrates the kingdom, representing the King (the Lord Jesus Christ) on one hand, and also the princes (14:8,9) who individually lead the 12 tribes. Possibly, he will be a descendant of David.[9]

We glean from Ezekiel 44-46 and 48 a few details about the enigmatic prince:

1. He worships the Lord (v. 46:2).
2. He cannot enter the sanctuary by the East Gate; it is reserved for the Lord alone (v. 44:3).
3. He is permitted to enter by the East Gate of the temple when he makes a special freewill offering to the Lord (v. 46:12).
4. He is given special sanction to enter and leave the sanctuary by way of the East Gate's vestibule (v. 44:3).
5. He may sit inside the east gateway of the temple sanctuary and eat of the sacrificial meal in the presence of the Lord (v. 44:3). No one else is permitted to do so.
6. He is not ordained to perform priestly duties (v. 46:2).

---

[9]John MacArthur, *The MacArthur Study Bible (NKJ)*, Word Publishing, 1997, p. 1216.

7. He is of royal personage and oversees the public offerings the people will make to the Lord during the appointed feast times (vv. 45:16-17, 22-25).

8. He is a model of integrity for the people he serves. He sets the tone and example of worship, drawing people closer to God (vv. 46:10-12).

9. Separate from the land portion set aside for the 12 tribes, the prince is allotted a section of property in two parts of the sacred city's holy district called the "district of the Lord." He lives and performs his duties within this district (vv. 45:1, 7).

10. His two-part parcel of land is equivalent to that of any one tribe (vv. 45:7, 48:21-22).

11. He will have biological sons of his own (vv. 46:16-18). By the way, other Scriptures indicate Christ will have a posterity (Is. 22:15-25, 53:10, 89:24-29), who will serve Him (Ps. 22:30, 45:16-17).

Glimpses into the Millennium

As we examine the role and duties of the prince in these chapters of Ezekiel, we are given some insight into how life will be during Christ's 1,000-year reign. Remarkably, the earth will not be free of sin. Everyone will not be a devoted follower of Messiah! For this reason, He will rule the nations with a "rod of iron" or "iron scepter" (Rev. 12:5a). Unlike in the past, no one who is "uncircumcised of the heart and flesh" will be allowed to enter the Lord's temple (Eze. 44:9). This reveals there will be people who are nonbelievers during Messiah's rule. They will be barred from entering the Lord's temple, and thus, defiling His sanctuary (Eze. 44:6-9).

In Ezekiel 45:9-12, the leaders (called "princes") of Israel's 12 tribes during Christ's reign are cautioned to be honest and forthright in their commercial dealings and transactions. The exhortation implies, under Messiah's rule, people will be fully capable of sin (e.g., covetous and greedy for gain).

We should understand there will be those on earth who escape God's judgment at His Second Coming because they believe in Christ. They survive the Great Tribulation. These believers will repopulate the earth during Christ's millennial reign. However, just because they are believers does not necessarily mean their children or their children's children will be believers. After multiple generations, there will be many who are not loyal to Christ.

After Christ's millennial reign, Satan will be released for a short while to deceive the nations. Rejecters of Christ will surely follow the Deceiver in his final rebellion against the King of kings (Rev. 20:7-9). Eternal damnation will be their final inheritance (Rev. 20:10).

Why Sacrifices in the Millennium?

One might ask, "Why should there be any kind of sacrifice or offering during the Millennium since Christ's perfect sacrifice on the cross for the sins of men obliterated that system?" We should view the offerings during this period as memorials. The Lord wants us to remember His appointed feasts (festivals) because they mark momentous milestones in the history of His people and mankind.

For example, there will always be an observance of Passover to remind future generations of what God did to free His people from Egypt's bondage. Again, we should view these sacrificial offerings, not as covering man's sins, but as remembrances of mankind's sin being, once and for all, covered. Of such offerings, John MacArthur's commentary brilliantly notes:

> *They are of a memorial nature; they are not efficacious any more than the Old Testament sacrifices were. As Old Testament sacrifices pointed forward to Christ's death, so these are tangible expressions, not competing with, but pointing back to the value of Christ's completely effective service, once for all (Heb. 9:28, 10:10). God at that time endorsed Old Testament offerings as tokens of forgiving and cleansing worshippers on the basis and credit of the great Lamb they pointed to, who alone could take away sins (John 1:29).[10]*

MacArthur goes on to explain, "*The bread and the cup, which believers today find meaningful, do not compete with Christ's cross, but are tangible memorials of its glory. So, will these sacrifices be.*"[11]

Prince Joshua clearly plays a vital role in the public administration of these commemorative tributes. He serves his Father, the King of kings. He also serves the 12 princes of Israel and the people.

---

[10]John MacArthur, *The MacArthur Study Bible (NKJ),* Word Publishing, 1997, p. 1215.
[11]Ibid.

Chapter Twelve
Joshua, Son of Jehozadak and Joshua, Son of Nun—Prototypes of the Lord's Joshua

Our Creator seems to take pleasure in communicating to us through shadows, types, and patterns. Frequently, a person, place, event, or nation that existed under the Old Covenant foreshadows a similar person, place, event, or nation under the New Covenant. That is, the original or prototype foreshadows something or someone important to come under the New Covenant of Jesus Christ. After His death and resurrection, Yeshua introduced a New Covenant between God and mankind, obliterating the old one. God began dealing with mankind through His Son, the Anointed One, the inheritor of the nations (Ps 2:2, 6-7).

The Old Testament shadow, type, or pattern usually points to a spiritual reality that conveys a truth or message that can only be discerned by those in whom God's Spirit dwells. A person must receive Jesus Christ as His Lord and Savior for God's Spirit to indwell him or her.

Shadows, types, and patterns—some spanning centuries and even millennia—are good teaching tools. They help discerning Bible students confirm truth or glimpse something or someone to come. Further, only God can orchestrate such phenomena:

- Joseph, as a suffering servant, was a type of Christ. He was rejected by his brothers and sold into slavery for 20 pieces of silver. Despite their rejection of him, God used Joseph to save his brothers and countless others. He was an Old Testament shadow of our Savior Jesus Christ, who was rejected by His brethren and sold for 30 pieces of silver.

- Moses, the deliverer of the children of Israel from Egypt's bondage, foreshadowed Christ, the Deliverer of mankind from sin and death's bondage.

- In Scripture, the world is cast as a place of oppression and subjugation—a type of Egypt. Canaan is cast as the "land of milk and honey" or the Promised Land—a type of heaven.

- The Great Exodus of the Old Testament foreshadowed a Greater Exodus to come—the rapture! At the rapture, God's people, covered by the Lamb's atoning blood, will escape God's judgment on the world (Egypt). Like the children of Goshen, they will escape the plagues God will pour on the nations.

- In the same manner the children of Israel inherited Canaan, God's chosen people will inherit heaven.

- King David was an Old Covenant shadow of Jesus Christ. Like King David, Christ will return as a Conquering King at His Second Coming. And like His ancestor David, He will rule and shepherd His people with wisdom and justice.

- The grandeur of Solomon's reign pointed to the splendor and majesty of the reign of the Greater Solomon to come—Yeshua Ha-Mashiach.

- Scripture clearly presents "The Madman," Antiochus IV Epiphanes, as the archetype for the future Antichrist (Dan. 11:21-32).

In early 2000, I discovered Joshua, the son of Jehozadak and leader of the Jewish exiles, to be an Old Testament type and cast of Yeshua and Joshua, His son. Under the Old Covenant, the predecessor's role and responsibilities to Israel point to a role Joshua will play as a chief magistrate over Israel's 12 tribes during Christ's millennial reign. As the prince, Joshua will have royal-civic duties specific to Israel as well as play a significant part in leading God's people in the worship of his Father.

January 2, 2000

More Revelations on Joshua

Quite unexpectedly today, the Lord showed me a type and cast of Himself and His son Joshua in the Old Testament book of Zechariah. Actually, He gave me this passage almost two years ago. But it held no meaning for me then because He had not yet revealed Joshua's name. However, this morning, the verses seized and riveted my attention:

> *Take the silver and gold and make a crown, and set it on the head of the high priest, Joshua son of Jehozadak. Tell him this is what the Lord Almighty says: "Here is the man whose name is the Branch, and he will branch out from his place and build the temple of the Lord. It is he who will build the temple of the Lord, and he will be clothed with majesty and will sit and rule on his throne (Zech. 6:11-13a, NIV).*

"Here is a man whose name is Branch …" is a clear reference to Yeshua. "He will branch out from this place …" indicates Christ, the

Branch, will start in Israel and He will expand, grow, generate, and produce, opening God's kingdom to Gentiles (v. 15). The phrase could also be a veiled reference to the Branch producing offspring or progeny. Surely, the "natural seed" (Joshua) of Messiah (the Branch) is an extension of Him. Further, the Son's son will produce sons of His own (Eze. 46:16-18, Psalm 45:16).

Interestingly, Isaiah 11:1 also speaks metaphorically of Christ being a rod, stem, and branch: "There shall come forth a Rod from the stem of Jesse, and a Branch shall grow out of his roots." In Isaiah's day, after the Babylonian captivity, it looked as if the Davidic line was finished. But Life (Messiah) sprang from its roots. What most people do not know in our generation is that the "Branch" shall have natural "branches" or "extensions" (i.e., offspring) of His own.

A deeper study of Zechariah revealed some notable similarities between Joshua, the son of Jehozadak, who was the first high priest, following Judah's Babylonian exile. He foreshadowed Christ, our King and High Priest, and His son to come:

Joshua Son of Jehozadak	Joshua Son of Yeshua
Joshua means Yeshua in Hebrew.	Joshua means Yeshua in Hebrew.
First high priest after the exiles' return (Hag. 1:1, Zech. 6:11).	Son of earth's first High Priest after final gathering of exiles (Heb. 4:14, 9:11).
Became leader over Israel after deported Jews returned from Babylonian exile (Zech. 3:1-8).	Becomes a leader of Israel's 12 tribes in the Millennium, after God's people are freed from Babylon the Great (Eze. 44-46, 48).
Crowned a royal governor over the returning Jewish exiles to depict Messiah's combined role of High Priest and King (Zech. 6:9-15).	Serves as a chief magistrate over Israel's 12 tribes as indicated by his two-part, tribe-size property allotment in Lord's holy district (Eze. 45:7, 48:21-22).

Joshua Son of Jehozadak	Joshua Son of Yeshua
Led the Jews in worship of God (Ez. 3:2; Zech. 6:11, 13).	Leads the 12 tribes in worship of the King of kings (Eze. 44:16-17a).
Had sons of his own (Neh. 12: 7, 26).	Has sons of his own (Eze. 46:16-18, Psalm 45:16).

Joshua, Son of Nun—Another Shadow of the Lord's Joshua

The best-known Joshua of the Bible led God's people into Canaan, the Promised Land after Moses' death. He was Moses' understudy and protégé. This Old Testament figure and what happened at the Battle of Jericho prefigured the Lord's son Joshua and what will happen during the Day of the Lord.

Joshua, Protégé of Moses and the Battle of Jericho	Joshua, Son of Yeshua and the Day of the Lord
Moses, a deliverer of God's people and mediator of the Old Testament Covenant, preceded Joshua, who was like a son to him.	Yeshua, a deliverer of God's people and mediator of the New Testament Covenant, preceded His son Joshua.
Joshua, son of Nun from the tribe of Ephraim, was born in Egypt and was delivered from there.	Joshua, son of Yeshua, will be born in the world, a type of Egypt, and he will be delivered from there. ("I call My son out of Egypt.")
Moses delivered God's chosen people from the bondage of Egypt, but he did not lead them into the Promised Land. Joshua led the children of Israel into the Promised Land.	Yeshua delivered God's elect from the bondage of sin and death, but He did not lead them, en masse, into the Promised Land (heaven). His son Joshua, caught up to His throne prior to the rapture as a sign to the church that she will follow, "leads" His corporate body into the Promised Land.

Joshua, Protégé of Moses and the Battle of Jericho	Joshua, Son of Yeshua and the Day of the Lord
God parted the Jordan River to allow His people to cross over into the Promised Land.	God will part the sky "in the twinkling of an eye" to allow His people to cross over into the Promised Land (heaven).
Christ, the Commander in Chief of the Lord's angels, appeared to Joshua before the Jericho battle in a rare "Christophany." He indicated He was set to lead Israel into victory, to possess the Promised Land (Jos. 5: 13-15). He and His angels warred in a realm not visible to the human eye.	Yeshua, our Commander in Chief and Ark of Safety in the Day of the Lord, leads us in our battle to possess the Promised Land (heaven)—individually at death and corporately at the rapture. He and His angels war for us the spirit realm, which is not visible to the human eye.
On the seventh day of the Jericho battle, God's army and seven priests marched around Jericho seven times, blowing seven trumpets.	In the Day of the Lord, Yeshua looses seven seals. The seventh seal releases seven trumpet blasts by seven angels, who release seven bowl judgments.
With a shout, Jericho's walls fell, which allowed God's people to take the city and ultimately enter the Promised Land.	With a shout, the voice of an arch angel and trumpet of God, Yeshua will free His people from the bondages of the world as they ascend to the Promised Land—heaven. (1 Thess. 4:16-18)
God shook and demolished the walls of Jericho, because Jericho kept His people from possessing the Promised Land. Afterward, the city and everything in it, was burned by fire.	In an epic earthquake, God will move every mountain and island on the face of the earth. He will demolish societies, institutions, systems, and infrastructures to help His people possess the Promised Land (heaven). Then, the nations of the world will be destroyed by fire.

Joshua, Protégé of Moses and the Battle of Jericho	Joshua, Son of Yeshua and the Day of the Lord
Only Rahab's family was saved from Jericho's destruction. She placed her faith in Israel's God when she tied a scarlet (red) cord to her window to signal her allegiance to Him and His people.	Only a remnant will be saved from the worldwide destruction to come—those who accept Christ's blood sacrifice for their sins. They signal their allegiance to Him when they accept His gift of salvation.
Nothing accursed of God was allowed to enter the Promised Land (Jos. 7:10-28).	Nothing accursed of God will be allowed to enter the Promised Land (heaven).
Joshua led the people in the worship of the Lord and the renewal of the Old Covenant after they entered the Promised Land.	Joshua will lead Israel's 12 tribes in the worship of the Lord during Christ's Millennial reign (Eze. 44:16-17a).
Joshua divided the land among the 12 tribes of Israel, and until his death, led Israel.	Joshua will serve as a chief magistrate over Israel's 12 tribes—each assigned to its own land—during Christ's Millennial reign (Eze. 44-46, 48).

Joshua and the Battle of Jericho serves as an opaque shadow of what God's people can expect during the Day of the Lord. Joshua, the Lord's son, will "lead" God's people into the ultimate Promised Land—heaven. As he is caught up to God's throne, he will precede Christ's corporate body. His birth and seizure from Satan's tentacles serve as a powerful sign to Christ's heaven-bound bride that she, too, will be snatched up.

Chapter Thirteen
Signs in the Heaven

Some believers view the concept of "signs in the heaven" as pagan superstition. However, there is an immense difference between astrology and astronomy. God Himself declared: *"Let there be lights in the firmament of the heavens to divide the day from night; and let them be for signs and seasons, and for days and years …." (Gen. 1:14, emphasis mine).* The Lord frequently employs celestial signs to forewarn His people of coming events and disasters. All invariably have a special connection to Israel, and thus, have the potential to shakeup the planet. Remember the bright star that led the wise men to the Christ Child? That star marked the birth of a little Jewish Baby destined to rule the world.

Similarly, the great Day of the Lord will be preceded by heavenly signs:

> *And it shall come to pass in the last days, says God, that I will pour out My Spirit on all flesh… I will show wonders in the heaven above and signs in the earth beneath … The sun shall turn into darkness, and the moon into blood, before the coming of the great and awesome day of the Lord (Acts 2:17a, 19-20).*

We are warned a "dark sun" and "red moon" will announce the Lord's return. They signal the age's end: *"I looked when He opened the sixth seal, and behold, there was a great earthquake; and the sun became black as sackcloth of hair, and the moon became like blood" (Rev. 6:12).* The Prophet Joel warns, *"The sun shall be turned into darkness, and the moon into blood, before the coming of the great and awesome day of the Lord"* (Joel 2:31).

The Significance of 1997/Hebrew Year 5758

God uses special solar and lunar eclipses and other celestial occurrences as heavenly billboards of coming events and disasters. It is significant that we witnessed blood-red and sackcloth moons over Jerusalem on March 23, 1997 during the Feast of Purim and on September 16, 1997 during the Days of Teshuva (Repentance). Curiously, 1997 was the Hebrew Year 5758, which means "Season of Noah." This is significant because the Lord warns His Second Advent will be like the days of Noah: *"But as the days of Noah were, so also will the coming of the Son of Man be" (Matt. 24:37).*

The Hale-Bopp Comet, the most-watched comet in history, appeared to earth residents only twice *ever*—once 4,200 ago and again in 1997. It arrived in the constellation of Argo, which means "ark" or "ship." The first time it appeared was to herald the Great Flood of Noah's day. It was a time of catastrophic worldwide judgment.

For those of us who can hear what the Spirit is saying, we know the heavenly wonder was a warning from above. The comet was a sign to our generation that we are fast approaching an extraordinary period akin to Noah's day—the Dreadful Day of the Lord. It, too, will be a time of worldwide judgment and will culminate with Christ's return!

In God's economy, timing is always significant. It is no coincidence that my strange and astonishing end-time journey with Him commenced in 1997/5758—the Season of Noah.

Additionally, all three fall feasts that year—Feast of Trumpets (Rosh Hashanah), Day of Atonement (Yom Kippur), and Feast of Tabernacles (Sukkot)—occurred in October—the same month the Lord visited me and planted the promise of Joshua in my womb. That year, the world entered a critical period. The Lord began setting the stage for the age's end and His appearing.

Intriguingly, October 31, 1997, the day the Lord deposited Joshua, was also Rosh Chodesh Cheshvan. Cheshvan marks the second month on the Jewish calendar, counting from Rosh Hashanah. Jews believe that the Great Flood began in Cheshvan. They are also taught Cheshvan is reserved exclusively for the time of Messiah, who will inaugurate the Third Temple in the month of Cheshvan during the Millennium.

Israel and the Four Red Moons

In 2014 *and* 2015, an extremely rare sequence of four, red-moon lunar eclipses (i.e., tetrad) is expected to occur on Passover *and* Feast of Tabernacles. Shall something tumultuous happen to Israel during those years or shortly thereafter? In heaven's eyes, Israel is the center of the world. Any disaster that touches her, the apple of God's eye, will reverberate throughout the world.

According to the Jewish Talmud, a lunar eclipse is a bad omen for Israel and Jewish people; a solar eclipse is a bad omen for the world. On March 20, 2015, a total solar eclipse is expected to occur. That celestial event is flanked by Passover and Feast of Tabernacles in 2014 *and* Passover and Feast of Tabernacles in 2015. Furthermore, red moons are expected to occur on all *four* feast days. This heavenly sequence has occurred only three other times in the last 500 years!

John Hagee—pastor, evangelist, and national chairman of Christians United for Israel—revealed each of those times aligned with a major historical (and violent) event for Israel. And each event carried significant implications for the world:

1. In 1492, Spain's monarchy signed a decree that stripped the Jews of their wealth and ejected them from its kingdom and territories. Tens of thousands of Jews were massacred.
2. In 1948, Israel became a nation.
3. In 1967, Israel reclaimed Jerusalem in the Six Day War.

Four hundred and fifty-six years after the Jews were ousted from Spain, Israel was reborn as a nation. This was after more than 1,900 years in exile! Seventeen years later, Israel supernaturally recaptured Jerusalem, her capital city, in a bloody six-day war. Could the tetrad sequence expected in 2014 and 2015 continue the pattern of securing Israel in her land? Will the Lord allow some cataclysmic event to occur in these years or shortly thereafter that will *forever* settle Israel's claim to the land He gave her through the Patriarchs, Abraham, Isaac, and Jacob?

Israel is surrounded by hostile forces that challenge her claim to the land. It is easy to see how a battle over this land, so sacred to God and His people, could escalate into a world war. Israel's enemies have vowed to wipe her off the face of the earth. In the Day of the Lord, God will surely weigh in and settle the matter, once and for all.

The Celestial Drama of Revelation 12

This brings us to the discussion of the celestial unfolding of Revelation 12. Many theological experts, Christian astronomers, and other ardent stargazers believe God has given our generation a dramatic preview of momentous events to come in a heavenly unfolding of Revelation 12. They believe He has written the Revelation story in the constellations. At the start of the chapter we are told, "Now a great sign appeared in heaven...."

Virgo (the "Virgin") or Bethulah (Hebrew name) represents Israel, who at or near *every* Feast of Trumpets (Rosh Hashanah), is "clothed with the sun." At that time, the moon can literally be seen "under her feet." In the past, a constellation of smaller stars (Coma Berenices) has been seen to form a crown of 12 stars atop her head, and Draco, the dragon, emerges just beneath the woman. She is about to give birth to the child (Jupiter). Draco appears to be in position to devour the child after he is born. The heavenly configuration dovetails with the Revelation 12 passage.

Using Scripture as a backdrop, many Bible scholars take this heavenly imagery (and other similar configurations) and attempt to calculate the time of the rapture or Christ's return. But no one knows the time of these events except God in heaven. It is this writer's belief that at some point on God's calendar, the appropriate and designated stars *will* align to create a flawless, heavenly billboard of the Revelation 12 story. It will signal to the discerning believer that something unprecedented is about to happen on earth. (I personally believe it will signal the *season* of Joshua's birth if not the specific day, just as the Star of Bethlehem heralded Christ's birth.) While we cannot know the exact date or time of the rapture or Christ's return, the heavenly sign will be a sure warning that we have entered the close of the age and cataclysmic times.

In March 1999, the Lord gave my friend and spiritual mentor, Suzanne Eustache, the strangest dream of all about Joshua and me. It may point to a heavenly spectacle to come, one that will unfold when Joshua and I are snatched away.

March 3, 1999

Suzanne's Dream: Heaven's Special Child

Suzanne called this morning. She was desperate to talk to me. But just as she began to speak the movers rang the doorbell. "Suzanne, I have to call you back. The movers are here," I explained.

I decided to part with most of our belongings upon learning Denny's paid nearly $50,000 to store our furniture last year. Michael's few things were shipped back to him in Chicago. And I gave away nearly everything I owned.

Ryan and I brought only a few items back to my parents' house. Unloading the warehouse took the entire day. I made a mental note to return Suzanne's call that night. We worked so hard and long that by evening every part of my body ached. I crashed into bed at 10:30 p.m. Only then did I remembered to call Suzanne; but it was too late. I knew she would be asleep. I'll call tomorrow I promised myself and drifted off to sleep.

Another day of unpacking boxes and distributing items to family and friends left me completely drained. Again, I failed to call. It was late the following night when I crawled into bed. I heard the Lord speak: "Call Suzanne tomorrow." It was a directive. I promised I would. I asked Him to remind me. The next day, just after 9 p.m., I finally called her. When I did, Suzanne recounted the most intriguing dream to me:

We were walking toward each other. I was coming from the west and you came from the east. You were beautifully attired in a blue-gray dress. Finally, we were face to face. But we never spoke. We simply looked at each other.

Suddenly, a lightning bolt came down from the sky and struck your stomach. It was in the shape of a star when it touched your belly. It was a brilliant star! The light from it began to grow. Slowly, it covered your entire body—everything but your face.

Then, you turned around and walked back the way you came. You never spoke a word. I watched you as you walked away. After a while, you disappeared. I woke up.

After a short while, I fell back to sleep. I had another dream. In the second dream, I tried three times to tell you about my first dream, but I kept getting interrupted. Every time I tried to tell you, someone pulled you away. Finally, I woke up.

Surely, Suzanne's second dream had already occurred. It served as a type of witness that her first one will also come to pass. She tried to tell me about her first dream the day she dreamt it, but the movers interrupted her. I promised I would call her back later that day, but I was too tired. I was not able to return her call the next day either. A third day would past before we spoke.

Few people know that I am pregnant in the Spirit. I know the child will be an exceptional boy. Suzanne's first dream certainly underscores that fact. He is heaven sent and I know heaven bound. Perhaps, when we are taken there will be unmistakable signs in the heavens. Discerning believers will know the Church's departure is imminent and Christ is at the door!

While I do not know the exact time Joshua and I will be taken, and no one knows the date or time of the rapture or of Christ's return, I do hold to the view that the Lord's Second Advent will coincide with Israel's fall feasts. His return will tie to Israel's fall feasts in the same way His First Advent corresponds to the spring feasts.

Feast of Trumpets is the next feast to be fulfilled. It marks the beginning of Israel's Civil New Year (Rosh Hashanah). It signifies a time of God calling His people together in solemn assembly to repent in preparation for His judgment. It is also a time of the blowing of the trumpets (or Shofar). In ancient times, the blowing of the Shofar warned God's people that war was imminent. It also signaled a bridegroom coming unexpectedly for his waiting bride.

God ordained seven feasts (or festivals) for the ancient Hebrews as lasting statutes to be practiced forever throughout their generations. Each of these appointed feasts is a holy convocation or sacred assembly. God ordained these seven feasts as "rehearsals" or "recitals" for His great plan to reveal the Messiah (Col. 2:16-17).

Hosea prophesied the Messiah's First and Second Advents would be like the "former and latter rains" (Hos. 6:3). The former rain ties to the four spring feasts, and the latter rain ties to three fall feasts. These Hebraic festivals point to Christ's two advents.

The first four feasts (or festivals) link to Christ's First Coming as the Suffering-Servant Savior. The Feast of Passover signified His sacrificial death as the Lord's Passover Lamb. The Feast of Unleavened Bread denoted His burial. The Feast of Firstfruits represented His resurrection. Pentecost symbolized the giving of the Holy Spirit.

The last three festivals—Feast of Trumpets (Rosh Hashanah), Day of Atonement (Yom Kippur), and Feast of Tabernacles (Sukkot)—point to Christ's Second Coming. At that time, He will come as the Triumphant Conquering Messiah. As the rightful heir to earth's throne, He will take back the planet from Satan, the Usurper.

During Feast of Trumpets (Rosh Hashanah), the Bridegroom will call His bride out of the world before He judges it. This is the blessed rapture! Day of Atonement points to a day of worldwide repentance after Christ is revealed to all as the True Messiah. Feast of Tabernacles looks forward to the time when Immanuel ("God with us") will "tabernacle" (i.e., live) with His people on earth in Jerusalem, the Holy City of God.

Chapter Fourteen
The Color of Love

I purposely saved the topic of race for last. If I could avoid it altogether, I would and just let everyone be delightfully surprised when God reveals all. But right now, it is the big elephant in the room. Everyone sees it and would like to pretend it is not there. But we kid ourselves.

We must acknowledge the topic and address it head on within the context of this book. I sense a need and an obligation to deal with it because of Joshua. Perhaps, we all will learn something significant about the Lord's perception of race and His observations of us as we grapple with our own preconceptions of people and people groups. If I were you, I would not want to be on the wrong side of this issue when I see the Lord face to face. If you are a blood-bought believer in Christ, you *will* see Him face to face and you will be without excuse for any bigotry you have practiced.

I was born and raised in the United States of America, so I know firsthand just how deep racial biases run in this country. For some, they are all-consuming. Although color prejudice can be found within every racial and ethnic group in our country, not everyone struggles with this demon.

Our nation's history makes it difficult for us to talk about race openly and honestly. Often, more is left unsaid than said. We are reluctant to speak our hearts for fear of being misunderstood. And to be honest, we have not explored one another's worlds enough to truly know what goes on in them. Furthermore, we have a common enemy who is hell bent on keeping us divided. Consequently, many of us rarely or never cross racial or ethnic lines. In the kingdom of God, it should not be that way for us. Love overrules everything. It trumps all.

In several dreams discussed in the book, Joshua appears to be a child of mixed racial heritage. Like the Shulamite, I am as dark as the "tents of Kedar" (So. of Sol.1:6). This is partly due to the hot Florida sun under which I toil most of my days. And it is partly due to genetics. I am of Ethiopian ancestry. Yet, in dreams Joshua is often seen as pale or light complexioned. Some have described him as "almost white."

Maybe my initial astonishment at his "almost white" skin tone is why God chose to conceal his color from me in many of my early dreams. Gradually, He permitted me to see more of him as time passed. Perhaps, this was after He developed in me a sure and deep-abiding color blindness, one that clearly shows in my day-to-day interactions with people.

After carefully reviewing the 32 dreams the Lord has given me about Joshua to date, I believe by American standards he would be considered racially mixed. Of course, this supposition leads to an even BIGGER elephant in the room! What must Christ look like?

For nearly 18 years, I have been on this phenomenal journey with the Lord, and He has presented Himself to me in countless dreams and visions. For many years, He purposely *never* let me see His face or detect His skin color. The creative maneuvers He employed to accomplish this were endless.

In later dreams and visions, I was permitted to see a full figure. However, the Figure *always* changed with each subsequent dream. He deliberately, intentionally altered His race, color, nationality, age, physical stature, and so on. Similarly, in the five divine encounters in which He came to me disguised as someone else, He differed radically in every imaginable way.

Moreover, I have had the privilege of seeing Mary, the mother of our Lord and Savior, in two dreams. In one dream, she was a stunningly beautiful Caucasian woman, sitting on a throne at the right hand of our Lord and Savior. At the sight of my big belly she greeted me excitedly and with open arms.

In the other dream, she appeared to be a gracious regal queen of African descent, who stood head and shoulders above everyone in the entire room. As He did with Himself, the Lord dramatically varied her appearance in the two dreams. Again, this was deliberate. He did it for a reason.

Historically, we know Christ is a Jew—a Semite, from the line of Shem. Therefore, He is neither Greek nor Roman, as medieval and Renaissance artists have portrayed Him. When Western civilization began to rise and take center stage in world affairs, the reimaging of Christ made Him appear more Western European than Middle Eastern. While this is not accurate—most scholars believe He should have an olive complexion versus a pale or ruddy appearance—God does not want us to get hung up on skin color.

It is no coincidence that the Bible distinguishes people and people groups based on national identity and ethnic tribes, not by race. Have you ever wondered why there is no mention of skin color in the Bible? We *never* see color distinctions made in Scripture because color prejudice did not exist then as it does today. A reference to a people being either Semitic or Hamitic did not necessarily denote the peoples' color or racial heritage. Rather, it signified a people who shared a common ancestral heritage, cultural lifestyle, and language.

For example, a Semite and a Hamite represented two different ancestral lines. However, a Semite—a descendant from the ancestral line of Shem, Noah's first son (and from whom the Patriarchs Abraham, Isaac, and Jacob originated) could be as dark as a Hamite. A Hamite was the progeny of Noah's second son, Ham. (Japheth was Noah's third son.)

Interestingly, Scripture reveals that the ancient Hebrews—descendants of Shem—were often mistaken for Egyptians, who were descendants of Ham, a dark-skinned people. For example, Joseph's brothers believed he was a native Egyptian when they sought food in Egypt during the famine (Genesis 42:1-8). The entire company—Hebrew and Egyptian—that buried Jacob in Canaan were mistaken for Egyptians (Genesis 50:7-11). Moses was mistaken for an Egyptian by the priest of Midian's seven daughters (Exodus 2:19). Even the Apostle Paul was mistaken for an Egyptian by Claudias Lysias, the commander of the Roman garrison (Acts 21:38).

In heaven and at the onset of the Millennium, there will be no color or racial prejudice. These biases are a construct of Satan to divide people. However, because the world will not be sin-free during Christ's 1000-year reign, it is highly conceivable that generations of nonbelievers will fall back into the color trap. Regardless, God's people will be one in Him. Yes, there will be people of diverse colors and races, but color and race will not matter. In early 2009, the Lord demonstrated this to me in a dream He gave me about Joshua:

February 28, 2009

A Dream: An Odd Family ... A Super Baby Boy

The dream opens with me in a home filled with all kinds of people who do not seem to go together. But they are one big family—all related. I see people who appear to be Caucasian and people who appear to be of African descent. A woman begins introducing me to one and all. Everyone wants me to meet one special lady. They all gather around, waiting for her to appear.

Finally, she arrives, accompanied by two other women. She looks like an African queen! She is extraordinarily tall, like a giant. (This feature usually denotes the person is of eminent stature in heavenly realms.) The two women on either side of her are much shorter. She smiles and hugs me close. The instant we embrace, I become her height! The scene changes.

Next, I find myself sitting in a pool chair on a screened patio. I see a shirtless, elderly Caucasian man with a gut, running on the deck of a swimming pool. He suddenly drops his pants to reveal a pair of pleated, khaki swimming trunks. He jumps in the swimming pool and shouts something. (I believe he yells "Marco Polo," a name used in a pool game that kids play.)

At that point, I turn to my right to see the most darling little boy. He is only about five years old and laughing with pure delight. The child has fair skin and curly, sandy hair. He could be white or of a mixed-race heritage. He appears related to the old man. Clearly, they have played this game before.

Suddenly, the little boy grabs a long barbell off the wall. It is loaded with a full set of weights! Laughing, the child lifts the barbell over his head, walks to the end of the pool like a little Hercules, and prepares to dive in. I freeze. I am certain I am watching an accident in the making!

The child holds the barbell with both hands above his head. Without a doubt, the right end of the barbell is going to hit the pool's metal stair railing when he jumps in. He is much too close to it. Just before he jumps into the pool, the barbell flips into a vertical position and slides smoothly into the water. The youngster, laughing with all his heart, has no idea the accident that just had been averted.

Once in the pool, the little man-child discovers a big, black fireman's hose and a large black fireman's hat. The force of the water gushing from the rubber hose causes it to snake wildly back and forth and up and down. The child, in his shiny fireman's hat, grabs hold of the hose. Up and down and around he goes. I am horrified. His little head bobs and convulses, but he will not let go of the hose! Surely, he is going to kill himself! Finally, he masters the hose into a still position. He laughs throughout the ordeal.

In the next scene, Ryan appears next to me. We both are wearing swimsuits. I am standing to get a better view of all the activity going on with this kid. I am apprehensive about what he will do next.

My Millennial Family

Clearly, the second part of the dream is about Joshua—a super baby, the son of a true Superman. I now suspect the old man in the swimming trunks is the Lord in yet another disguise.

In the dream, Joshua appears to have supernatural might and a tenacity that matches His Father's. Perhaps, the strength he demonstrates indicates he will be especially gifted and determined. I certainly suspect that which takes others much longer to figure out or master, will come easily to him because he is the Lord' son. But, is it also possible that the unusual strength he displays in the dream is meant to convey he will have supernatural abilities like his Father?

One thing is very apparent to me—the boy is wild, crazy, and totally fearless. Consistent with other dreams the Lord has given me about Joshua, he seems to be a handful for me. Frequently, I am seen fretting over his safety because of his wild behavior and because he is the Lord's child.

In the first part of the dream, the odd family is my new blended family in heaven or during the Millennium. In real life, my family is comprised mostly of African Americans. But my heavenly/millennial family will be a mélange of at least two different races. Together, as one family, we may look peculiar to many of earth's present-day residents. But in the dream, skin color is not an issue for anyone. No one notices or speaks of it, which is how it should be.

The Spirit of the Lord just spoke to me! The giant woman in my dream is Mary, the mother of Yeshua! This makes sense, as the dream is about Christ's son (who I am to bear) and Mary (who bore Him). Surely, she is revered in heaven more than she is on earth. Notably, once again, God has tied both of us together—the two women symbolizing Israel in Revelation 12.

The Lord has gone to great lengths to present Himself as the Savior of *all* people and a King who will rule the nations with justice and righteousness. I can only conclude one thing. The color of His blood is far more important than the color of His skin!

His blood is red. Our blood is red. Because the Lamb's blood is red, we are saved by His sacrifice. He poured Himself out for *every* race, nationality, ethnic group, tribe, and tongue. He has no prejudice. This is a Man-God, who allowed three Canaanite women—one a former prostitute—to become a part of His genealogy (Matthew 1:3, 5, 6).

The color of our skin matters not to Him. *"For the Lord does not see as man sees; for man looks at the outward appearance, but the Lord looks at the heart" (1 Sam. 16:7b).* He desires we do the same. The Lord's chief concern is that we are covered by His blood and dressed in His white robe of righteousness at His return. Otherwise, we cannot enter His eternal kingdom. End of debate. End of story.

Epilogue

I have thought a lot about Mary, the mother of our Lord and Savior, Jesus Christ. Just imagine. The Creator of the universe allowed Mary, a created being, to carry Him in her womb for nine months. Shielded in this quiet place, she supported and nourished Him. Then, she gave birth to Him—God! The boundless, all-powerful Living Word chose to confine and limit Himself to a tiny, microscopic Seed inside a mortal woman's womb. That Seed formed into an Embryo, and then later, into a helpless human Infant. Into a desperately cruel and wicked world, He came as a vulnerable little Baby.

How extraordinary it must have been for Mary to be the one chosen to love and raise this precious Child. How she must have marveled at God's inscrutable ways as she held Him in her arms. What could she have possibly pondered in her heart as she played with His little fingers? (These were the fingers of God!) How her soul must have leapt when she caressed His tiny face, kissed His soft cheeks. What was it like to watch God laugh, to watch Him sleep?

At the same time, I think how marvelous, remarkable, and wondrous God must be to entrust Himself to a fallible human being. But He went a step further. Mary was an inexperienced young mother, married to a man of no power or means. Surely, this mattered not to God. A pure heart was all He required.

I am both amazed and humbled by a God who would allow Himself to be nursed, cuddled, and cooed by an imperfect mortal. God conceived and initiated this astounding plan, not man. Who are we that He cares so much?

As I try to put myself in Mary's place, it all seems inconceivable until I remember God's motive, the reason He willingly chose to leave the majesty and splendor of heaven to become what He became. God desired to save us from our wretchedness. He knew we could not save ourselves. His desire was to restore us and the earth to Himself. So, He made an amazing sacrifice—a mindboggling, honorable, noble sacrifice.

Now imagine the Creator as a grown man in all His glory, about to receive a son of His own. Again, He chose to use an imperfect, mortal woman. I think of Mary—who she was and all she must have thought and experienced as she raised her Son, our Savior.

As I think of her, I can no longer be perplexed and dumbfounded by the staggering revelations the Lord has shown me about His own son and His plans for him. It is as mystifying and mysterious as His own birth. For years, I have been blown away by it all. I found it too incredible to believe. But no longer. Nothing is impossible with God.

SELECTED BIBILOGRAPHY

Hagee, John. *Four Blood Moons*. Nashville, Tennessee: Worthy Publishing, 2013.

Hurnard, Hannah. *Hinds' Feet on High Places*. Wheaton, Illinois: Tyndale House Publishers, Inc., 1975.

MacArthur, John. *The MacArthur Study Bible*. Nashville, Tennessee: Word Publishing, 1997.

McDowell, Josh and Steward, Don. *Understanding the Cults: Handbook of Today's Religions*. Nashville, Tennessee: Thomas Nelson Publishers, 1996.